Global Issues in Employment Discrimination Law

By

Samuel Estreicher
Dwight D. Opperman Professor of Law
New York University Law School

Brian Landsberg
Professor of Law
University of the Pacific, McGeorge School of Law

AMERICAN CASEBOOK SERIES®

THOMSON
WEST™

Mat #40541665

610 Opperman Drive
St. Paul, MN 55123
1–800–313–9378

Printed in the United States of America

ISBN: 978–0–314–17607–3

TEXT IS PRINTED ON 10% POST CONSUMER RECYCLED PAPER

For the Roses in my life—

Rose Abramowicz Estreicher (1917–2004)

Hannah Rose Estreicher (neé May 17, 1987)

Sophia Rose Estreicher (neé July 1, 2006)

—S.E.

For my former colleagues in the Civil Rights Division, U.S. Department of Justice, pioneers in enforcing the fair employment laws.

—B.L.

*

Preface

The aim of this book is to develop materials that would supplement a basic course in employment discrimination law or serve a special seminar. The focus throughout is on the issues and developments that a well-informed U.S. employment lawyer needs to keep abreast of different approaches to the regulation of employment discrimination in today's increasingly integrated world economy.

Although occasionally an article or book excerpt seemed a more efficient vehicle, we have tried in most places to introduce the student to primary materials, whether agency or court decisions, statutes or regulations. Even though the concerns of employment discrimination law now properly transcend the borders of the U.S., we remain lawyers who must be able to solve clients' problems and navigate policy dilemmas with the skills and habits of our craft.

The idea of enacting laws to forbid various forms of discrimination in employment is often thought of as American in origin. And it is true that laws against race discrimination began with U.S. executive orders banning employment discrimination by federal contractors and developed their modern form with the adoption of the Civil Rights Act of 1964 and the later interpretation of Reconstruction legislation to reach private racial discrimination by employers. However, the Treaty of Rome in 1957, establishing the principle that women employed in the European Union must receive equal pay for equal work, preceded the U.S. Equal Pay Act by six years. The years since have seen a vast expansion of the employment discrimination laws, both in the United States and elsewhere. Laws forbidding employment discrimination based on disability, age, national origin, religion, alien status, and sexual identity have in many countries been added to the laws against race and sex discrimination.

Some 4,060 U.S. firms now operate over 63,200 branches, subsidiaries and affiliates in 191 countries, with sales of over $10 trillion. 1 Directory of American Firms Operating in Foreign Countries, introduction (19th ed. 2007). We can expect more employment discrimination issues to grow in number and complexity as U.S. employers increasingly operate abroad, foreign employers increasingly operate in the U.S., and workers from within and outside the U.S. increasingly cross national lines to pursue employment. Most countries now have adopted laws forbidding various forms of employment discrimination. Often the laws of more than one country will apply to the employment relationship. While the overall thrust of the laws may be similar, their details differ. Moreover, in cases brought by U.S. employees working abroad for U.S. employers, the employment discrimination law of the United States applies only if compliance with U.S. law would not violate the law of the other country. Employment lawyers must often become familiar with the laws of other countries in order to provide sound advice to their clients.

Not only is some basic familiarity with the laws of other countries important to practitioners representing multinational employers or their employees, it also helps lawyers and scholars better understand the regluation of employment discrimination. Differences in the ways that other nations treat such issues as burdens of proof, comparable worth, sexual harassment, and relief can help us to evaluate the policies underlying the legal regime, as well as assess the impact of various rules.

While some Employment Discrimination casebooks offer occasional references to international law and the law of other countries, such references are the exception, not the rule. Our objective in this small volume is to provide a global law supplement that can be used with any of the casebooks. We do not attempt comprehensive coverage, but we hope we have rendered enough of the related institutional detail to give the reader exposure to the full range of issues and legal materials.

A note on the excerpting process used. Where substantive material is being deleted, this is indicated by a set of three asterisks. To minimize the distraction of these symbols, no indication is given where citations are being deleted or where a reading begins or ends in the original. Where the reader will have difficulty obtaining access to the original, a website is provided.

This book could not have been completed without the patient guidance of our wives, Aleta and Dorothy, respectively.

S.E. AND B.L.

November 2007

Acknowledgments

We would like to thank the authors and copyright holders of the following works:

Samuel Estreicher, Unjust Dismissal Laws: Some Cautionary Notes, 33 Am. J. Comp. L. 310 (1985)

Hiroya Nakakubo, "Phase III" of the Japanese Equal Employment Opportunity Act, 4 Japan Labor Rev. 9 (2007)

Anna Torriente, Minimum Employment Standards in Mexico, National Law Center for Inter-American Free Trade, Sept. 1995

Voices Against Discrimination: Chinese Citizens Challenge Discriminatory Practice, China Law and Governance Review, June 2004

*

Global Issues Series

Series Editor, Franklin A. Gevurtz

Titles Available Now

Global Issues in Civil Procedure by Thomas Main, University of the Pacific, McGeorge School of Law
ISBN 978–0–314–15978–6

Global Issues in Constitutional Law by Brian K. Landsberg, University of the Pacific, McGeorge School of Law and Leslie Gielow Jacobs, University of the Pacific, McGeorge School of Law
ISBN 978–0–314–17608–0

Global Issues in Contract Law by John A. Spanogle, Jr., George Washington University, Michael P. Malloy, University of the Pacific, McGeorge School of Law, Louis F. Del Duca, Pennsylvania State University, Keith A. Rowley, University of Nevada, Las Vegas, and Andrea K. Bjorklund, University of California, Davis
ISBN 978–0–314–16755–2

Global Issues in Corporate Law by Franklin A. Gevurtz, University of the Pacific, McGeorge School of Law
ISBN 978–0–314–15977–9

Global Issues in Criminal Law by Linda Carter, University of the Pacific, McGeorge School of Law, Christopher L. Blakesley, University of Nevada, Las Vegas and Peter Henning, Wayne State University
ISBN 978–0–314–15997–7

Global Issues in Employment Discrimination Law by Samuel Estreicher, New York University School of Law and Brian K. Landsberg, University of the Pacific, McGeorge School of Law
ISBN 978–0–314–17607–3

Global Issues in Employment Law by Samuel Estreicher, New York University School of Law and Miriam A. Cherry, University of the Pacific, McGeorge School of Law
ISBN 978–0–314–17952–4

Global Issues in Family Law by Ann Laquer Estin, University of Iowa College of Law and Barbara Stark, Hofstra University School of Law
ISBN 978–0–314–17954–8

Global Issues in Labor Law by Samuel Estreicher, New York University School of Law
ISBN 978–0–314–17163–4

Global Issues in Legal Ethics by James E. Moliterno, College of William & Mary, Marshall-Wythe School of Law and George Harris, University of the Pacific, McGeorge School of Law
ISBN 978–0–314–16935–8

Global Issues in Property Law by John G. Sprankling, University of the Pacific, McGeorge School of Law, Raymond R. Coletta, University of the Pacific, McGeorge School of Law, and M.C. Mirow, Florida International University College of Law
ISBN 978–0–314–16729–3

Global Issues in Tort Law by Julie A. Davies, University of the Pacific, McGeorge School of Law and Paul T. Hayden, Loyola Law School, Los Angeles
ISBN 978–0–314–16759–0

*

Summary of Contents

*

Table of Contents

*

Table of Cases

The principal cases are in bold type. Cases cited or discussed in the text are roman type. References are to pages. Cases cited in principal cases and within other quoted materials are not included.

Global Issues in Employment Discrimination Law

*

Chapter One

COVERED EMPLOYERS

Fair employment laws apply to domestic employers who fit within a statutory definition. In addition, the question arises whether they apply to employers who operate outside the country or to foreign employers who operate within the country.

A. U.S. EMPLOYERS ABROAD

EEOC v. ARABIAN AMERICAN OIL CO.

499 U.S. 244 (1991)

Justice Rehnquist delivered the opinion of the Court.

Petitioner Boureslan is a naturalized United States citizen who was born in Lebanon. The respondents are two Delaware corporations, Arabian American Oil Company (Aramco), and its subsidiary, Aramco Service Company (ASC). Aramco's principal place of business is Dhahran, Saudi Arabia, and it is licensed to do business in Texas. ASC's principal place of business is Houston, Texas. In 1979, Boureslan was hired by ASC as a cost engineer in Houston. A year later he was transferred, at his request, to work for Aramco in Saudi Arabia. Boureslan remained with Aramco in Saudi Arabia until he was discharged in 1984. After filing a charge of discrimination with the Equal Employment Opportunity Commission (EEOC or Commission), he instituted this suit in the United States District Court for the Southern District of Texas against Aramco and ASC. He sought relief under both state law and Title VII of the Civil Rights Act of 1964, 78 Stat. 253, as amended, 42 U. S. C. §§ 2000e—2000e–17, on the ground that he was harassed and ultimately discharged by respondents on account of his race, religion, and national origin. Respondents filed a motion for summary judgment on the ground that the District Court lacked subject-matter jurisdiction over Boureslan's claim because the protections of Title VII do not extend to United States citizens employed abroad by American employers. The District Court agreed and dismissed Boureslan's Title VII claim; it also dismissed his state-law claims for lack of pendent jurisdiction and entered final judgment in favor of respondents. [The U.S. Court of Appeals] for the Fifth Circuit affirmed. * * *

Both parties concede, as they must, that Congress has the authority to enforce its laws beyond the territorial boundaries of the United States. Cf. Foley Bros., Inc. v. Filardo, 336 U.S. 281, 284–285 (1949); Benz v. Compania Naviera Hidalgo, S. A., 353 U.S. 138, 147 (1957). Whether Congress has in fact exercised that authority in this case is a matter of statutory construction. It is our task to determine whether Congress intended the protections of Title VII to apply to United States citizens employed by American employers outside of the United States. It is a longstanding principle of American law "that legislation of Congress, unless a contrary intent appears, is meant to apply only within the territorial jurisdiction of the United States." *Foley Bros.*, 336 U.S., at 285. This "canon of construction ... is a valid approach whereby unexpressed congressional intent may be ascertained." Ibid. It serves to protect against unintended clashes between our laws and those of other nations which could result in international discord. See McCulloch v. Sociedad Nacional de Marineros de Honduras, 372 U.S. 10, 20–22 (1963). In applying this rule of construction, we look to see whether "language in the [relevant Act] gives any indication of a congressional purpose to extend its coverage beyond places over which the United States has sovereignty or has some measure of legislative control." *Foley Bros.*, supra, at 285. We assume that Congress legislates against the backdrop of the presumption against extraterritoriality. Therefore, unless there is "the affirmative intention of the Congress clearly expressed," *Benz*, supra, at 147, we must presume it "is primarily concerned with domestic conditions." *Foley Bros.*, supra, at 285. * * *

Petitioners' reliance on Title VII's jurisdictional provisions also finds no support in our case law; we have repeatedly held that even statutes that contain broad language in their definitions of "commerce" that expressly refer to "foreign commerce" do not apply abroad. For example, in New York Central R. Co. v. Chisholm, 268 U.S. 29 (1925), we addressed the extraterritorial application of the Federal Employers' Liability Act (FELA), 45 U. S. C. § 51 et seq. FELA provides that common carriers by railroad while engaging in "interstate or foreign commerce" or commerce between "any of the States or territories and any foreign nation or nations" shall be liable in damages to its employees who suffer injuries resulting from their employment. § 51. Despite this broad jurisdictional language, we found that the Act "contains no words which definitely disclose an intention to give it extraterritorial effect," *Chisholm*, supra, at 31, and therefore there was no jurisdiction under FELA for a damages action by a United States citizen employed on a United States railroad who suffered fatal injuries at a point 30 miles north of the United States border into Canada. Similarly, in McCulloch v. Sociedad Nacional de Marineros de Honduras, 372 U.S. 10 (1963), we addressed whether Congress intended the National Labor Relations Act (NLRA), 29 U. S. C. §§ 151–168, to apply overseas. Even though the NLRA contained broad language that referred by its terms to foreign commerce, § 152(6), this Court refused to find a congressional intent to apply the statute abroad because there was not "any specific language" in the Act reflecting congressional intent to do so. *McCulloch*, supra, at 19. * * *

Petitioners argue that Title VII's "alien exemption provision," 42 U. S. C. § 2000e–1, "clearly manifests an intention" by Congress to protect United States citizens with respect to their employment outside of the United States. The alien-exemption provision says that the statute "shall not apply to an employer with respect to the employment of aliens outside any State." Petitioners contend that from this language a negative inference should be drawn that Congress intended Title VII to cover United States citizens working abroad for United States employers. There is "no other plausible explanation [that] the alien exemption exists," they argue, because "if Congress believed that the statute did not apply extraterritorially, it would have had no reason to include an exemption for a certain category of individuals employed outside the United States." Brief for Petitioner in No. 89–1838, pp. 12–13. Since "the statute's jurisdictional provisions cannot possibly be read to confer coverage only upon aliens employed outside the United States," petitioners conclude that "Congress could not rationally have enacted an exemption for the employment of aliens abroad if it intended to foreclose all potential extraterritorial applications of the statute." Id., at 13.

Respondents resist petitioners' interpretation of the alien-exemption provision and assert two alternative raisons d'être for that language. First, they contend that since aliens are included in the statute's definition of employee, and the definition of commerce includes possessions as well as "States," the purpose of the exemption is to provide that employers of aliens in the possessions of the United States are not covered by the statute. Thus, the "outside any State" clause means outside any State, but within the control of the United States. Respondents argue that "this reading of the alien exemption provision is consistent with and supported by the historical development of the provision" because Congress' inclusion of the provision was a direct response to this Court's interpretation of the term "possessions" in the Fair Labor Standards Act in Vermilya–Brown Co. v. Connell, 335 U.S. 377 (1948), to include leased bases in foreign nations that were within the control of the United States. Brief for Respondents 27. They conclude that the alien-exemption provision was included "to limit the impact of *Vermilya–Brown* by excluding from coverage employers of aliens in areas under U.S. control that" were not encompassed within Title VII's definition of the term "State." Id., at 29.

Second, respondents assert that by negative implication, the exemption "confirms the coverage of aliens in the United States." Id., at 26. They contend that this interpretation is consistent with our conclusion in Espinoza v. Farah Mfg. Co., 414 U.S. 86 (1973), that aliens within the United States are protected from discrimination both because Title VII uses the term "individual" rather than "citizen," and because of the alien-exemption provision.

If petitioners are correct that the alien-exemption clause means that the statute applies to employers overseas, we see no way of distinguishing in its application between United States employers and foreign employers. Thus, a French employer of a United States citizen in France would be subject to Title VII—a result at which even petitioners balk. The EEOC assures us that in its view the term "employer" means only "American employer," but there is no such distinction in this statute and no indication that the EEOC in the normal course of its administration had produced a reasoned basis for such a distinction. Without clearer evidence of congressional intent to do so than is contained in the alien-exemption clause, we are unwilling to ascribe to that body a policy which would raise difficult issues of international law by imposing this country's employment-discrimination regime upon foreign corporations operating in foreign commerce.

This conclusion is fortified by the other elements in the statute suggesting a purely domestic focus. The statute as a whole indicates a concern that it not unduly interfere with the sovereignty and laws of the States. See, e. g., 42 U. S. C. § 2000h–4 (stating that the Act should not be construed to exclude the operation of state law or invalidate any state law unless inconsistent with the purposes of the Act); § 2000e–5 (requiring the EEOC to accord substantial weight to findings of state or local authorities in proceedings under state or local law); § 2000e–7 (providing that nothing in Title VII shall affect the application of state or local law unless such law requires or permits practices that would be unlawful under Title VII); §§ 2000e–5(c), (d), and (e) (provisions addressing deferral to state discrimination proceedings). While Title VII consistently speaks in terms of "States" and state proceedings, it fails even to mention foreign nations or foreign proceedings.

Similarly, Congress failed to provide any mechanisms for overseas enforcement of Title VII. For instance, the statute's venue provisions, § 2000e–5(f)(3), are ill-suited for extraterritorial application as they provide for venue only in a judicial district in the State where certain matters related to the employer occurred or were located. And the limited investigative authority provided for the EEOC, permitting the Commission only to issue subpoenas for witnesses and documents from "any place in the United States or any Territory or possession thereof," 29 U. S. C. § 161, incorporated by reference into 42 U. S. C. § 2000e–9, suggests that Congress did not intend for the statute to apply abroad. It is also reasonable to conclude that had Congress intended Title VII to apply overseas, it would have addressed the subject of conflicts with foreign laws and procedures. In amending the Age Discrimination in Employment Act of 1967 (ADEA), 81 Stat. 602, as amended, 29 U. S. C. § 621 et seq., to apply abroad, Congress specifically addressed potential conflicts with foreign law by providing that it is not unlawful for an employer to take any action prohibited by the ADEA "where such practices involve an employee in a workplace in a foreign country, and compliance with [the ADEA] would cause such employer . . . to violate the laws of the country in which such workplace is located." § 623(f)(1). Title VII, by contrast, fails to address conflicts with the laws of other nations.

[Eds. Congress responded to *Arabian American Oil* by amending Title VII in § 109 of the Civil Rights Act of 1991 ("§ 109" or "1991 amendments"). A similar provision is found in the employment title of the ADA, 42 U.S.C. §§ 12111–12117.]

TITLE VII OF THE CIVIL RIGHTS ACT OF 1964–1991 AMENDMENTS

42 U.S.C. 2000e–1 [§ 702]

(a) This subchapter shall not apply to an employer with respect to the employment of aliens outside any State * * *.

(b) It shall not be unlawful under section 703 or 704 [§§ 2000e–2 or 2000e–3 of this title] [the substantive provisions forbidding employment discrimination and retaliation] for an employer (or a corporation controlled by an employer) * * * to take any action otherwise prohibited by such section, with respect to an employee in a workplace in a foreign country if compliance with such section would cause such employer (or such corporation), such organization, such agency, or such committee to violate the law of the foreign country in which such workplace is located.

(c)(1) If an employer controls a corporation whose place of incorporation is a foreign country, any practice prohibited by section 703 or 704 [§§ 2000e–2 or 2000e–3 of this title] engaged in by such corporation shall be presumed to be engaged in by such employer.

(2) Sections 703 or 704 [§§ 2000e–2 or 2000e–3 of this title] shall not apply with respect to the foreign operations of an employer that is a foreign person not controlled by an American employer.

(3) For purposes of this subsection, the determination of whether an employer controls a corporation shall be based on—

(A) the interrelation of operations;

(B) the common management;

(C) the centralized control of labor relations; and

(D) the common ownership or financial control, of the employer and the corporation.

[Eds. In addition, the 1991 Act amended the definition of "employee" in 42 U.S.C. § 2000e(f) to include: "With respect to employment in a foreign country, such term includes an individual who is a citizen of the United States."]

Notes and Questions

1. **"Internal Affairs" of Foreign–Flag Ships in U.S. Waters**. In Spector v. Norwegian Cruise Line Ltd., 545 U.S. 119, 130–32 (2005), the Supreme Court held that the public accommodations title of the Americans with Disabilities Act (ADA) applied in part to foreign-flag cruise ships in U.S. waters:

> This Court has long held that general statutes are presumed to apply to conduct that takes place aboard a foreign-flag vessel in United States territory if the interests of the United States or its citizens, rather than interests internal to the ship, are at stake. * * * The general rule * * * is subject only to a narrow exception. Absent a clear statement of congressional intent, general statutes may not apply to foreign-flag vessels insofar as they involve only the internal order and discipline of the vessel, rather than the peace of the port. * * *
>
> This narrow clear statement rule is supported by sound principles of statutory construction. It is reasonable to presume Congress intends no interference with matters that are primarily of concern only to the ship and the foreign state in which it is registered. It is also reasonable, however, to presume Congress does intend its statutes to apply to entities in United States territory that serve, employ, or otherwise affect American citizens, or that affect the peace and tranquility of the United States, even if those entities happen to be foreign-flag ships.

> Cruise ships flying foreign flags of convenience offer public accommodations and transportation services to over 7 million United States residents annually, departing from and returning to ports located in the United States. Large numbers of disabled individuals, many of whom have mobility impairments that make other kinds of vacation travel difficult, take advantage of these cruises or would like to do so. To hold there is no Title III protection for disabled persons who seek to use the amenities of foreign cruise ships would be a harsh and unexpected interpretation of a statute designed to provide broad protection for the disabled.

The Court ruled that one aspect of the ADA concerning physical access to barriers on board could be viewed as "relating to the internal affairs of foreign-flag cruise ships"—particularly if ADA required required non-compliance with treaty obligations—and hence non-applicable in the absence of a clear statement from Congress.

2. **"Extraterritorial" Application?** Although extraterritorial application of Title VII, the Age Discrimination in Employment Act (ADEA) and the ADA are now governed by specific statutory provisions, other federal laws are still subject to analysis under *Arabian American Oil*. This will initially require a determination whether an "extraterritorial application" of the statute is being sought. Assume, for example, Boureslan had been transferred to work for Aramco in Saudi Arabia for only a temporary two-year assignment (what is often termed a "secondment"). Would his place of employment still be in the U.S., or would it now be in Saudi Arabia? Would we have a "workplace in a foreign country" within the meaning of amended § 702?

3. **Rationale for Extraterritorial Application?** What is the rationale for extending U.S. fair employment law extraterritorially? Note that one of the early and very colorful cases, Kern v. Dynalectron Corp., 577 F.Supp. 1196 (N.D. Tex. 1983), involved decisions made at Dynalectron's American headquarters regarding employment in Saudi Arabia. Kern was to fly helicopters to Mecca. Dynalectron required him to convert to Islam, because under Saudi law the penalty for a non-Muslim who enters Mecca is death. Rather than holding that Title VII did not apply outside the United States, the court stated:

> There can be no question but that non-Moslem pilots stationed in Jeddah are not safe as compared to Moslem pilots. Therefore, Dynalectron's discrimination against non-Moslems in general, and Wade Kern specifically, is not unlawful since to hire Moslems exclusively for this job "is a bona fide occupational qualification reasonably necessary to the normal operation of that particular business," § 703(a) of Title VII. Notwithstanding the religious discrimination in this case, the Court holds and finds that the B.F.O.Q. exception is properly applicable.

Id. at 1201. Consider also the citations found in note 12 of the 1993 "Enforcement Guidance" issued by the Equal Employment Opportunities Commission (EEOC), the U.S. federal agency responsible for administering Title VII and other federal employment anti-discrimination statutes:

> 12. Cf. also Abrams v. Baylor College of Medicine, 581 F.Supp. 1570, 1576, 1577, 34 EPD ¶ 34,303 (S.D. Tex. 1984) (finding violation of Title VII where employer rejected Jewish applicants for rotation program in Saudi Arabia based merely on informal conversations with Saudi officials; "various gleaned impressions to the effect that the Saudis did not want any Jews in their country;" and a "paternalistic 'concern' for the safety of Jews traveling to Arab lands"), aff'd in relevant part, 805 F.2d 528, 41 EPD ¶ 36,682 (5th Cir. 1986); Fernandez v. Wynn Oil Co., 653 F.2d 1273, 1276–77, 26 EPD ¶ 32,060 (9th Cir. 1981) (stereotypes that South American clients would refuse to deal with female executive insufficient to provide BFOQ for sex discrimination in denying job to woman in United States).

Do these cases along with *Kern* make the case for extraterritorial application or do they argue for a presumption against such application?

1993 EEOC ENFORCEMENT GUIDANCE ON APPLICATION OF TITLE VII AND THE AMERICANS WITH DISABILITIES ACT TO CONDUCT OVERSEAS

* * *

(available www.eeoc.gov/policy/docs/extraterritorial-vii-ada.html)

1. *Assessing the Nationality of Employers*

An initial question to be addressed in investigating charges of overseas discrimination therefore * * * is whether the entity that allegedly discriminated—or that controls the entity that allegedly discriminated—is an American employer.

Neither Section 109 nor its legislative history sets forth an explicit test for determining the nationality of employers. As an initial matter, however, investigators should look to a company's place of incorporation in ascertaining an employer's nationality. * * * Where a respondent is incorporated in the United States, it will typically be deemed to be an American employer because an entity that chooses to enjoy the legal and other benefits of being incorporated here must also take on the concomitant obligations. In many cases, therefore, the nationality of an entity will be relatively easy to discern.

Nonetheless, it may sometimes be necessary to examine factors beyond (or in lieu of) the employer's place of incorporation. For example, other factors will have to be weighed to assess the nationality of those entities (such as law firms or accounting partnerships) that are "employers" or other covered entities within the meaning of Title VII or the ADA, but that are not incorporated companies. Moreover, where the discriminating entity is incorporated outside the United States but has numerous contacts here, investigators may need to review the totality of that company's contacts with the United States to make a nationality termination.

Potentially relevant factors for assessing an entity's nationality include, but are not limited to: (a) the company's principal place of business, i.e., the place where primary factories, offices, or other facilities are located; (b) the nationality of dominant shareholders and/or those holding voting control; and (c) the nationality and location of management, i.e., of the officers and directors of the company. In situations such as those described in the above paragraph, a company may be found to be American if these factors suggest a significant connection to the United States. The factors must be considered on a case-by-case basis, and no one factor is determinative; generally, the greater the number of factors that demonstrate an entity's connection to the United States, the more reasonable a conclusion that it is an American employer.

* * *

2. Assessing "Control" by an American Employer

Even if an entity is not itself American, its discriminatory conduct overseas will be covered if it is "controlled" by an American employer. * * * Section 109 sets forth four factors to be considered in assessing whether such control exists. * * *

One case that discusses [these factors] specifically in the context of a Title VII claim against a foreign subsidiary of an American parent is Lavrov v. NCR Corp., 600 F. Supp. 923, 37 EPD ¶ 35,401 (S.D. Ohio 1984). Relying on the four factors now incorporated into Section 109, the *Lavrov* court found that there was sufficient evidence of the possible interrelationship of the American parent and its foreign subsidiary to justify a trial on the question. The court first determined that the foreign entity, which was a wholly owned subsidiary of the American company, shared common ownership with it. 600 F. Supp. at 928. The court treated as relevant evidence of the centralization of labor relations the facts that the American company instituted corporation-wide personnel policies; that certain personnel decisions with regard to individual employees required approval by the American company; and that the foreign subsidiary was not authorized to change any remuneration plans, benefits, or operating conditions without prior approval of its American parent. Id. The court also pointed to the American company's appointment of management members of the foreign subsidiary's board, and to the foreign company's function to market products assigned by the American company, as factors relevant to assessing, respectively, the commonality of management and the interrelationship of operations of the two companies. Id. * * *.

In discussing the evidence it found relevant, the *Lavrov* court also indicated that " 'all four criteria [for assessing integrated status] need not be present in all cases' " and that " 'the presence of any single factor in the Title VII context is not conclusive.' " 600 F. Supp. at 927 (citations omitted). * * *. The determination of whether nominally separate entities are an integrated enterprise will depend on the facts of each case.

* * *

C. The "Foreign Laws Defense" of Section 109 of the Civil Rights Act of 1991

Section 109 makes clear that "it shall not be unlawful," under either Title VII or the ADA, for an employer to take otherwise prohibited action if compliance with either statute, with respect to an employee in a workplace in a foreign country, would cause an employer to violate the law of the foreign country in which the workplace is located. * * *

Under this provision, a respondent must prove three elements to establish a foreign laws defense: that (1) the action is taken with respect to an employee in a workplace in a foreign country, where (2) compliance with Title VII or the ADA would cause the respondent to violate the law of the foreign country, (3) in which the workplace is located. * * *

1. *Employee in a Foreign Workplace*

To make out a foreign laws defense, an employer must first demonstrate that the challenged practice relates to an employee in a "workplace in a foreign country." Thus, the defense is unavailable under Title VII for employment practices that involve employees in any of the 50 States, the District of Columbia, Puerto Rico, the Virgin Islands, American Samoa, Guam, Wake Island, the Canal Zone, or the Outer Continental Shelf Lands as defined in the Outer Continental Shelf Lands Act. See Title VII, Section 701(i) (defining "State"); see also 29 C.F.R. § 1630.2 (d) (1992) (defining "State" for purposes of ADA jurisdiction).

2. *Violate the Law of the Foreign Country*

a. *Existence of a Law*

An employer must next prove that compliance with Title VII or the ADA would "cause" it to "violate the law of the foreign country." Under this prong of the defense, a respondent must initially demonstrate that the source of authority on which it relies constitutes a foreign "law." * * *

The court in Mahoney v. RFE/RL, Inc., 818 F. Supp. 1, 60 EPD ¶ 41,959 (D.D.C. 1992), identified * * * such circumstances in a case involving the ADEA foreign laws defense. In *Mahoney*, the defendant, an American employer, terminated plaintiffs, U.S. citizens working in Germany, based on a union contract that expressly required mandatory retirement at age 65. Defendant first claimed that the union contract, and the German labor practices it incorporated, were German "laws" that would be violated were defendant forced to comply with the ADEA. The court rejected this argument, holding that the defendant's union contract, although "legally binding," was not "law" for purposes of the ADEA foreign laws defense; the mandatory retirement provision had not been mandated by the German government and did not have general applicability beyond the parties to the contract. Id. at 3–4. Noting that "[t]he ADEA is a remedial statute and exceptions to it are to be construed narrowly," id. at 3, the court further held that foreign "[p]ractices and policies, even when embodied in contracts, are not 'laws' " for purposes of the defense. Id.

> The court also refused to treat as foreign "law" German court decisions enforcing the union contract. As noted by the court, the German court decisions did not hold that anything in German law compelled the decisions reached.... If overseas employers could avoid application of the ADEA simply by embedding an age-discriminatory provision in a contract, having a foreign court enforce the contract, and calling the court's decision "law," then the Act's extraterritorial provisions would be largely nullified, for employers could easily contract around the law. Id. at 5 (emphasis in original). Although the case was decided under the ADEA and applicable therefore to charges arising under that statute, the reasoning of *Mahoney* is equally applicable to analysis of the foreign laws defense under Title VII and the ADA.). * * *

b. "Cause" a Violation

Under the second prong of the foreign laws defense, an employer must also demonstrate that compliance with Title VII or the ADA would "cause" it to violate foreign law, i.e., that it is impossible to comply with both sets of requirements. * * * The defense will be established only where compliance with Title VII or the ADA will inevitably lead to a violation of foreign law. Cf. Kern v. Dynalectron Corp., 577 F. Supp. 1196, 33 EPD ¶ 34,194 (N.D. Tex. 1983) (employer had BFOQ defense for requiring helicopter pilots it employed in Saudi Arabia to convert to Moslem religion where Saudi Arabian law provided for beheading of non-Moslems who entered holy area), aff'd, 746 F.2d 810, 40 EPD ¶ 36,317 (5th Cir. 1984). * * *

3. *Where the Workplace is Located*

The final element of a successful foreign laws defense is proof that the foreign laws involved are those of the country in which the charging party's workplace is (or, absent the discrimination, would be) located. The laws of the country in which an employer is headquartered or incorporated would not control for purposes of this element of the defense unless the charging party's workplace is also located in that country.

Notes and Questions

1. **U.S. as Preferable Forum?** As we will see in the succeeding chapters, other nations are beginning to enact legislation similar to U.S. anti-discrimination laws. Germany, Japan, Mexico, and the United Kingdom and a host of other countries now also prohibit certain forms of discrimination and sexual harassment by legislation or judicial decision. Because liability under foreign labor laws for damages for discriminatory employment practices falls far short of the generous jury verdict awards obtainable in many U.S. jurisdictions, plaintiffs who have the choice may elect to bring their suit in the U.S. courts.

2. **Viability of Global HR Policies?** Should an employer apply its personnel policies dealing with harassment and discrimination to its overseas locations, even in situations where such conduct is not illegal? This is a very difficult business issue with concomitant legal consequences. Some would argue that in order to be competitive in foreign markets in which they conduct business, U.S. corporations cannot afford to extend the protections and rights embodied in U.S. employment discrimination laws to foreign nationals in overseas branches. According to this viewpoint, a company would violate its duty to its own shareholders if it extended such rights to foreign nationals under U.S. law on a voluntary basis. On the other hand, some would urge that voluntary compliance with U.S. employment discrimination laws makes good business sense—everyone ought to have the right to work in an environment which is free of discrimination or harassment regardless of citizenship, and any conduct to the contrary would detract from the reputation the company wants to enjoy wherever it does business.

3. **Inviting Claims of "Control" by U.S. Parent?** The EEOC's Enforcement Guidance takes the position that in assessing "control" of a foreign entity by an American employer for purposes of liability under the Civil Rights Act of 1964, "centralized control of labor relations" is the most important factor in determining whether the acts of the foreign employer are imputable to the U.S. employer. The agency cited Lavrov v. NCR Corp., 600 F.Supp. 923 (S.D. Ohio 1984), where the court found that there was sufficient evidence of an interrelation between an American parent corporation (NCR) and its

wholly-owned German subsidiary (NCR GmbH) to justify a trial discrimination against the U.S. parent for alleged discrimination committed by its foreign subsidiary.

Although increased control by a U.S. corporation over the personnel practices of branches and suppliers in a foreign country may increase exposure under U.S. employment discrimination law, it may also be essential to preventing costly and embarrassing misconduct that may harm the corporation's brand. Moreover, to the extent a multinational corporation maintains consistent personnel practices and rules designed to prevent on-the-job harassment and discrimination, employment law exposure can be controlled and reduced.

4. **Rights of Non–U.S. Citizens Working Abroad**? Although U.S. employment discrimination laws apply extraterritorially to protect U.S. citizens working abroad (for U.S. companies or U.S–controlled foreign corporations), non-U.S. citizens have no such legal rights. Under Title VII's alien clause, the statute does not apply "to an employer with respect to the employment of aliens outside any State." 42 U.S.C. § 2000e–1(a). Thus, while a U.S. citizen would have a Title VII right to be free of sexual harassment while working for a U.S.-controlled entity in Russia, a Russian citizen would have no such legal right. Nor would a U.S. permanent resident working for a U.S. controlled entity in Russia. See Shekoyan v. Sibley International, 409 F.3d 414, 422 (D.C. Cir. 2005):

> Shekoyan relies on the Immigration and Nationality Act, 8 U.S.C. § 1101, which defines "alien" to include "any person not a citizen or national of the United States," id. § 1101(a)(3), to support his interpretation that a national should not fall within Title VII's "alien" exclusion for overseas employees. Yet even assuming, *arguendo*, that a lawful permanent resident qualifies as as a U.S. national * * * Shekoyan faces a significant problem: Title VII does more that merely exclude an alien employed overseas from protection; it affirmatively grants protection only to a "citizen of the United States." 42 U.S.C. § 2000e(f). * * *
>
> Shekoyan's alternative argument, that he was not employed "in a foreign country" within the meaning of Title VII, 42 U.S.C. 2000e(f), is based on the facts that he was hired and trained in the United States, that many decisions related to his employment were made in the United States and that his letter of termination was sent to his Washington, D.C. residence. Because the employment letter contract between Sibley and Shekoyan stated Shekoyan's place of employment as "Tbilisi, Republic of Georgia" and classified him as "long-term personnel living in Georgia" and because Shekoyan resided and worked in Georgia throughout his employment with Sibley, however, we agree with the district court hat Shekoyan was engaged in "employment in a foreign country."

B. FOREIGN EMPLOYERS: THE ROLE OF TREATY

SUMITOMO SHOJI AMERICA, INC. v. AVAGLIANO

457 U.S. 176 (1982)

Chief Justice Burger delivered the opinion of the Court.

I

Petitioner, Sumitomo Shoji America, Inc., is a New York corporation and a wholly owned subsidiary of Sumitomo Shoji Kabushiki Kaisha, a Japanese general trading company or sogo shosha. Respondents are past and present female secretarial employees of Sumitomo. All but one of the respondents are United States citizens; that one exception is a Japanese citizen living in the United States. Respondents brought this suit as a class action claiming that Sumitomo's alleged practice of hiring only male Japanese citizens to fill executive, managerial, and sales positions violated . . . Title VII of the Civil Rights Act of 1964 * * *.

Without admitting the alleged discriminatory practice, Sumitomo moved under Rule 12(b)(6) of the Federal Rules of Civil Procedure to dismiss the complaint. The court refused to dismiss the Title VII claims; it held that because Sumitomo is incorporated in the United States it is not covered by Article VIII(1) of the [Friendship, Commerce and Navigation Treaty between the United States and Japan, Apr. 2, 1953, [1953] 4 U. S. T. 2063, T. I. A. S. No. 2863]. The District Court then certified for interlocutory appeal to the Court of Appeals under 28 U. S. C. § 1292(b) the question of whether the terms of the Treaty exempted Sumitomo from the provisions of Title VII.

The Court of Appeals reversed in part. The court first . . . concluded that the Treaty parties intended Article VIII(1) to cover locally incorporated subsidiaries of foreign companies such as Sumitomo. The court then held that the Treaty language does not insulate Sumitomo's executive employment practices from Title VII scrutiny. The court concluded that under certain conditions, Japanese citizenship could be a bona fide occupational qualification for high-level employment with a Japanese-owned domestic corporation and that Sumitomo's practices might thus fit within a statutory exception to Title VII. The court remanded for further proceedings.

We granted certiorari, 454 U.S. 962 (1981), and we vacate and remand.

II

Interpretation of the Friendship, Commerce and Navigation Treaty between Japan and the United States must, of course, begin with the language of the Treaty itself. The clear import of treaty language controls unless "application of the words of the treaty according to their obvious meaning effects a result inconsistent with the intent or expectations of its signatories." Maximov v. United States, 373 U.S. 49, 54 (1963). See also The Amiable Isabella, 6 Wheat. 1, 72 (1821).

Article VIII(1) of the Treaty provides in pertinent part:

> "[C]ompanies of either Party shall be permitted to engage, within the territories of the other Party, accountants and other technical experts, executive personnel, attorneys, agents and other specialists of their choice."[6]

Clearly Article VIII(1) only applies to companies of one of the Treaty countries operating in the other country. Sumitomo contends that it is a company of Japan, and that Article VIII(1) of the Treaty grants it very broad discretion to fill its executive, managerial, and sales positions exclusively with male Japanese citizens.[7]

Article VIII(1) does not define any of its terms; the definitional section of the Treaty is contained in Article XXII. Article XXII(3) provides:

6. Similar provisions are contained in the Friendship, Commerce and Navigation Treaties between the United States and other countries. See, e. g., Article XII(4) of the Treaty with Greece, [1954] 5 U. S. T. 1829, 1857, T. I. A. S. No. 3057 (1951); Article VIII(1) of the Treaty with Israel, [1954] 5 U. S. T. 550, 557, T. I. A. S. No. 551 (1951); Article VIII(1) of the Treaty with the Federal Republic of Germany, [1956] 7 U. S. T. 1839, 1848, T. I. A. S. No. 3593 (1954).

These provisions were apparently included at the insistence of the United States; in fact, other countries, including Japan, unsuccessfully fought for their deletion. * * * According to Herman Walker, Jr., who at the time of the drafting of the Treaty served as Adviser on Commercial Treaties at the State Department, Article VIII(1) and the comparable provisions of other treaties were intended to avoid the effect of strict percentile limitations on the employment of Americans abroad and "to prevent the imposition of ultranationalistic policies with respect to essential executive and technical personnel." Walker, Provisions on Companies in United States Commercial Treaties, 50 Am. J. Int'l L. 373, 386 (1956); Walker, Treaties for the Encouragement and Protection of Foreign Investment: Present United States Practice, 5 Am. J. Comp. L. 229, 234 (1956). According to the State Department, Mr. Walker was responsible for formulation of the postwar form of the Friendship, Commerce and Navigation Treaty and negotiated several of the treaties for the United States. * * * See also Foreign Service Despatch No. 2529, supra, App. 182a (Purpose of Article VIII(1) of Treaty with Germany "is to preclude the imposition of 'percentile' legislation. It gives freedom of choice as among persons lawfully present in the country and occupationally qualified under the local law").

7. The issues raised by this contention are clearly of widespread importance. As we noted in n. 6, supra, treaty provisions similar to that invoked by Sumitomo are in effect with many other countries. In fact, some treaties contain even more broad language. See, e. g., Article XII(4), Treaty of Friendship, Commerce and Navigation with Greece, [1954] 5 U. S. T., at 1857–1859 ("Nationals and companies of either party shall be permitted to engage, within the territories of the other Party, accountants and other technical experts, executive personnel, attorneys, agents and other employees of their choice ...") (emphasis added). As of 1979, United States affiliates of foreign corporations employed over 1.6 million workers in this country. * * *

> "As used in the present Treaty, the term 'companies' means corporations, partnerships, companies and other associations, whether or not with limited liability and whether or not for pecuniary profit. Companies constituted under the applicable laws and regulations within the territories of either Party shall be deemed companies thereof and shall have their juridical status recognized within the territories of the other Party."

Sumitomo is "constituted under the applicable laws and regulations" of New York; based on Article XXII(3), it is a company of the United States, not a company of Japan. As a company of the United States operating in the United States, under the literal language of Article XXII(3) of the Treaty, Sumitomo cannot invoke the rights provided in Article VIII(1), which are available only to companies of Japan operating in the United States and to companies of the United States operating in Japan.

The Governments of Japan and the United States support this interpretation of the Treaty. Both the Ministry of Foreign Affairs of Japan and the United States Department of State agree that a United States corporation, even when wholly owned by a Japanese company, is not a company of Japan under the Treaty and is therefore not covered by Article VIII(1). * * *

The United States Department of State also maintains that Article VIII(1) rights do not apply to locally incorporated subsidiaries. Although not conclusive, the meaning attributed to treaty provisions by the Government agencies charged with their negotiation and enforcement is entitled to great weight. Kolovrat v. Oregon, 366 U.S. 187, 194 (1961).[11]

Our role is limited to giving effect to the intent of the Treaty parties. When the parties to a treaty both agree as to the meaning of a treaty provision, and that interpretation follows from the clear treaty language, we must, absent extraordinarily strong contrary evidence, defer to that interpretation.

III

Sumitomo maintains that although the literal language of the Treaty supports the contrary interpretation, the intent of Japan and the United States was to cover subsidiaries regardless of their place of incorporation. We disagree.

Contrary to the view of the Court of Appeals and the claims of Sumitomo, adherence to the language of the Treaty would not

11. Determining the nationality of a company by its place of incorporation is consistent with prior treaty practice. See Walker, 50 Am. J. Int'l L., supra n. 6, at 382–383. The place-of-incorporation rule also has the advantage of making determination of nationality a simple matter. On the other hand, application of a control test could certainly make nationality a subject of dispute.

"overlook the purpose of the Treaty." The Friendship, Commerce and Navigation Treaty between Japan and the United States is but one of a series of similar commercial agreements negotiated after World War II. The primary purpose of the corporation provisions of the Treaties was to give corporations of each signatory legal status in the territory of the other party, and to allow them to conduct business in the other country on a comparable basis with domestic firms. * * *

The Treaties accomplished their purpose by granting foreign corporations "national treatment"[18] in most respects and by allowing foreign individuals and companies to form locally incorporated subsidiaries. These local subsidiaries are considered for purposes of the Treaty to be companies of the country in which they are incorporated; they are entitled to the rights, and subject to the responsibilities, of other domestic corporations. By treating these subsidiaries as domestic companies, the purpose of the Treaty provisions—to assure that corporations of one Treaty party have the right to conduct business within the territory of the other party without suffering discrimination as an alien entity—is fully met.

Nor can we agree with the Court of Appeals view that literal interpretation of the Treaty would create a "crazy-quilt pattern" in which the rights of branches of Japanese companies operating directly in the United States would be greatly superior to the right of locally incorporated subsidiaries of Japanese companies. The Court of Appeals maintained that if such subsidiaries were not considered companies of Japan under the Treaty, they, unlike branch offices of Japanese corporations, would be denied access to the legal system, would be left unprotected against unlawful entry and molestation, and would be unable to dispose of property, obtain patents, engage in importation and exportation, or make payments, remittances, and transfers of funds. Ibid. That this is not the case is obvious; the subsidiaries, as companies of the United States, would enjoy all of those rights and more. The only significant advantage branches may have over subsidiaries is that conferred by Article VIII(1).

IV

We are persuaded, as both signatories agree, that under the literal language of Article XXII(3) of the Treaty, Sumitomo is a company of the United States; we discern no reason to depart from the plain meaning of the Treaty language. Accordingly, we hold

18. "National treatment" is defined in Article XXII(1) of the Treaty:

> "The term 'national treatment' means treatment accorded within the territories of a Party upon terms no less favorable than the treatment accorded therein, in like situations, to nationals, companies, products, vessels or other objects, as the case may be, of such Party." * * *

that Sumitomo is not a company of Japan and is thus not covered by Article VIII(1) of the Treaty.[19] The judgment of the Court of Appeals is vacated, and the case is remanded for further proceedings consistent with this opinion.

Notes and Questions

1. **Application to Age Bias?** *Sumitomo* left many unresolved questions. For example, in MacNamara v. Korean Air Lines, 863 F.2d 1135, 1140–41 (3d Cir. 1988), MacNamara, a U.S. citizen, was dismissed by Korean Air Lines (KAL) after having worked for them as a district sales manager for several years. His dismissal was allegedly part of a reduction in force in which six U.S. managers were discharged and replaced by four Korean citizens. In explaining why MacNamara's ADEA claim could go forward, the Court of Appeals stated:

> Because we agree with KAL that MacNamara's replacement was an "executive" within the meaning of Article VIII(1) [of the Friendship, Commerce and Navigation Treaty with Korea] and that the right "to engage" foreign nationals necessarily includes the right to replace people in MacNamara's position with a foreign national, we must wrestle with the broader issues * * *.
>
> * * * Article VIII(1) goes beyond securing the right to be treated the same as domestic companies in that its purpose, in part, is to assure foreign corporations that they may have their business in the host country managed by their own nationals if they so desire. We also agree * * * that Article VIII(1) was not intended to provide foreign businesses with shelter from any law applicable to personnel decisions other than those that would logically or pragmatically conflict with the right to select one's own nationals as managers *because of their citizenship*. Insofar as Title VII and the ADEA proscribe intentional discrimination on the basis of race, national origin, and age, we perceive no theoretical or practical conflict between them and the right conferred by Article VIII(1). Thus, for example, we believe that a foreign business may

19. We express no view as to whether Japanese citizenship may be a bona fide occupational qualification for certain positions at Sumitomo or as to whether a business necessity defense may be available. There can be little doubt that some positions in a Japanese controlled company doing business in the United States call for great familiarity with not only the language of Japan, but also the culture, customs, and business practices of that country. However, the Court of Appeals found the evidentiary record insufficient to determine whether Japanese citizenship was a bona fide occupational qualification for any of Sumitomo's positions within the reach of Article VIII(1). Nor did it discuss the bona fide occupational qualification exception in relation to respondents' sex discrimination claim or the possibility of a business necessity defense. Whether Sumitomo can support its assertion of a bona fide occupational qualification or a business necessity defense is not before us.

We also express no view as to whether Sumitomo may assert any Article VIII(1) rights of its parent.

not deliberately undertake to reduce the age of its workforce by replacing older Americans with younger foreign nationals.

2. **Other Open Issues**. Other open issues are discussed in the EEOC's 1993 Enforcement Guidance:

1993 EEOC ENFORCEMENT GUIDANCE ON APPLICATION OF TITLE VII AND THE AMERICANS WITH DISABILITIES ACT (CONTINUED FROM EXCERPT ON P. 8)

It is well settled that, absent constraints imposed by treaty or by binding international agreement, Title VII applies to a foreign employer when it discriminates within the United States. * * * By employing individuals within the United States, a foreign employer invokes the benefits and protections of U.S. law. As a result, the employer should reasonably anticipate being subjected to the Title VII enforcement process should any charge of discrimination arise directly from the business the employer does in the United States. * * *

A. Types of Agreements and Treaties that May Affect the Coverage of Title VII or the ADA

Although Title VII and the ADA may be generally applicable when a charge challenges discrimination by a foreign or foreign owned employer within the United States, such a respondent may allege that it is protected by the terms of a treaty or international agreement that limits the full applicability of U.S. anti-discrimination laws. * * *

B. Assessing Whether a Respondent is Protected by a Treaty

When a respondent invokes the protections of a treaty or agreement the first question is whether the respondent is covered by the specific treaty at issue. * * *

In *Sumitomo*, the Supreme Court held that the FCN treaty between the United States and Japan did not exempt wholly owned American subsidiaries of Japanese companies from Title VII. * * *

It should be noted, however, that *Sumitomo* does not resolve all issues of treaty interpretation. First, the Supreme Court in *Sumitomo* was construing the language of a particular FCN treaty. The Court expressly reserved judgment on whether a similar interpretation would apply to FCN treaties between the United States and other countries, reasoning that other treaties, "although similarly worded, [might] have different negotiating histories." 457 U.S. at 185 n.12. * * *

Second, the Seventh Circuit has stated that *Sumitomo* left open the question whether an American subsidiary might assert any of its parent's treaty rights where there was a contention that the parent had dictated the subsidiary's discriminatory conduct. Fortino v. Quasar Co., 950 F.2d 389, 393 (7th Cir. 1991) (citing *Sumitomo*, 457 U.S. at 189–90 n.19). The *Fortino* court held that an American-incorporated subsidiary of a Japanese parent company may in such circumstances assert the FCN treaty rights of its parent, "at least to the extent necessary to prevent the treaty from being set at naught." 950 F.2d at 393. In *Fortino*, Quasar, a division of a U.S.-incorporated company owned by a Japanese corporation, discharged its American executives and gave preferential treatment to executives sent temporarily to the United States by the Japanese parent. According to the court, a judgment refusing to apply the U.S./Japanese FCN treaty and thereby "forbid[ding] Quasar to give preferential treatment to the expatriate executives that its parent sends would have the same effect on the parent as it would have if it ran directly against the parent; it would prevent [the parent] from sending its own executives to manage Quasar in preference to employing American citizens in these posts." Id.

The Commission disagrees with the result in *Fortino* and believes that permitting a U.S. subsidiary of a Japanese corporation to assert its parent's treaty rights enables that subsidiary " 'to accomplish indirectly what it cannot accomplish directly [under the holding in *Sumitomo*].' " Spiess v. C. Itoh & Co. (America), Inc., 725 F.2d 970, 973, 33 EPD ¶ 34,213 (5th Cir. 1984) (quoting unpublished order denying motion to dismiss) * * * As a result, in charges filed outside the Seventh Circuit, the Commission will continue to treat place of incorporation as determinative of the FCN treaty protection to which Japanese-owned companies are entitled. * * *

C. Assessing Whether Employment Practices Are Covered by a Treaty

If a respondent is covered by a treaty, the next question to be addressed is whether the treaty applies to the employment practices challenged in the charge. As with issues of coverage discussed * * * above, the answer depends on the facts of the charge and on the language and intent of the specific treaty at issue.

* * *

In assessing whether treaty protection is available, investigators should look first to the job as to which discrimination is alleged to have occurred. A job title or label may not be determinative; investigators should identify actual job functions and the charging party's relationship to others of the respondent's employees. In addition, investigators should consider the relationship between the treaty and the action an employer is alleged to have taken. A treaty permitting an employer to "engage" certain personnel of its choice is, for example, probably applicable not only to a charge of discriminatory hiring but also to one of unlawful discharge. Compare [MacNamara v. Korean Air Lines, 863 F.2d 1135, 1141–42 (3d Cir. 1988) (right to "engage" executives under Korean FCN treaty includes right to terminate current personnel and replace them with executives who share defendant's nationality). However, such a treaty may be inapplicable if the charge challenges wage discrimination. But see Spiess v. C. Itoh & Co. (America), Inc., 643 F.2d 353 (5th Cir. 1981) (applying treaty right to "engage" executives to case challenging company's policy of restricting promotions and benefits to Japanese citizens), vacated on other grounds, 457 U.S. 1128 (1982). * * *

D. Assessing the Protection Granted by a Treaty

If a respondent can invoke treaty protections that cover the challenged employment practice, the final question to be addressed is the impact of the treaty on the application of Title VII or the ADA. Like other issues of coverage, this question ultimately depends on the language of the particular treaty at issue and on the intent of the treaty parties.

In general, FCN treaty provisions will control to the extent that they permit discriminatory conduct that would otherwise violate Title VII. See, e.g., *Spiess*, 643 F.2d at 356 ("unless federal civil rights laws reflect an affirmative disavowal of the rights provided by [a] Treaty, it is our duty to implement the treaty rights"); *MacNamara*, 863 F.2d at 1146 ("in the absence of evidence suggesting Congress intended subsequent legislation to affect existing treaty rights, and in the event the enactments conflict, the Treaty must prevail"). Even broadly worded treaties will not, however, "entitle a foreign company operating in the United States to select among American citizens on the basis of their age, race, sex, religion, or national origin." *MacNamara*, 863 F.2d at 1143; see also Wickes v. Olympic Airways, 745 F.2d 363, 365, 35 EPD ¶ 34,676 (6th Cir. 1984) (U.S./Greek FCN treaty "was intended to be a narrow privilege to employ Greek *citizens* for certain high level positions, not a wholesale immunity from compliance with labor laws prohibiting other forms of employment discrimination") (emphasis in original).

Most courts construing the scope of particular FCN treaties have further determined that the protection they extend is only the right of foreign companies covered by the treaty to prefer citizens of their own countries for executive, management, and other identified positions. See, e.g., *Spiess*, 643 F.2d at 359 (U.S./Japanese FCN treaty exempts covered companies "from domestic employment discrimination laws to the extent of permitting discrimination in favor of Japanese citizens in employment for executive and technical positions"); *Wickes*, supra, 745 F.2d at 365; *MacNamara*, 863 F.2d at 1140 (U.S./Korean FCN treaty intended to shelter foreign businesses from "any law ... that would logically or pragmatically conflict with the right to select one's own nationals as managers *because of their citizenship*") (emphasis in original). * * *

> Example: Tubu, Ltd., is a Tubistian company doing business in the United States. Under an FCN treaty between Tubistan and the United States, Tubistian companies operating in the United States are authorized to hire Tubistian citizens for executive positions. CP, a U.S. citizen of German origin, charges that he has been denied such a position in favor of a Venezuelan citizen. Tubu asserts the FCN treaty as a defense.
>
> Tubu's treaty defense is likely to fail because the treaty authorizes preferences only for Tubistian citizens. In this case, Tubu has preferred a Venezuelan citizen. While Tubu's conduct may ultimately be found not to violate Title VII, Tubu cannot rely on the treaty as a defense.

See Starrett v. Iberia Airlines, 756 F. Supp. 292, 295 (S.D. Tex. 1989).

Courts have also addressed the relationship between Title VII and a treaty that grants the right to prefer citizens. In *MacNamara*, for example, the Third Circuit determined that the U.S./Korean FCN treaty protected the right of a covered company to prefer its own citizens, but only *because of their citizenship.* As a result, the court held that the treaty barred disparate impact challenges against the Korean defendant that were based simply on the defendant's requirement that employees have Korean citizenship. In contrast, the court held that the treaty did not shield the foreign employer from disparate treatment claims alleging that the employer had intentionally preferred Korean citizens because of their race, sex, national origin, religion, or age. 863 F.2d at 1140–48; see also Brief of the United States as *Amicus Curiae* on Petition and Cross–Petition for a Writ of Certiorari in Korean Air Lines v. MacNamara, Nos. 88–1449, 88–1551 (Sept. 1989) (approving Third Circuit's reasoning). Compare, e.g., Fortino v. Quasar Co., 950 F.2d at 393 (refusing to decide whether FCN treaty "confers a blanket immunity from Title VII" for claims of intentional discrimination on the basis of national origin), with Avigliano v. Sumitomo Shoji America, 638 F.2d 552, 559, 24 EPD ¶ 31,460 (2d Cir. 1981) (treaty does not insulate Japanese employer from Title VII, because Title VII, through the BFOQ defense, permits company to employ "Japanese nationals in positions where such employment is reasonably necessary to the successful operation of its business"), vacated on other grounds, 457 U.S. 176, 29 EPD ¶ 32,782 (1982), and Linskey v. Heidelberg Eastern, Inc., 470 F. Supp. 1181, 1186, 20 EPD ¶ 30,058 (E.D.N.Y. 1979) (U.S./Danish FCN treaty "was not intended to immunize foreigners from claims under the host country's employment discrimination laws").

C. EUROPEAN LAW ON EXTRATERRITORIAL APPLICATION

INGRID BOUKHALFA v GERMANY

[1996] ECR I-2253

[Eds. Germany employed a Belgian national in its Algerian embassy. Germany and Belgium both belong to the European Union [at the time called the European Community, but here referred to as EU], while Algeria does not. Germany applied in the Belgian national's case the rules governing non-German employees of the embassy, rather than the rules that govern German employees. She sued for a violation of EU provisions banning discrimination based on nationality, which are analogous to the U.S. Constitution, Art. IV, § 2 ("The Citizens of each State shall be entitled to all Privileges and Immunities of Citizens in the several States."). The court reasoned:]

13. It must be borne in mind that not only Article 48 of the Treaty but also regulations, as institutional acts adopted on the basis of the Treaty, apply in principle to the same geographical area as the Treaty itself (Case 61/77 Commission v. Ireland [1978] ECR 417, paragraph 46).

14. The geographical application of the Treaty is defined in Article 227. That article does not, however, preclude Community rules from having effects outside the territory of the Community.

15. The Court has consistently held that provisions of Community law may apply to professional activities pursued outside Community territory as long as the employment relationship retains a sufficiently close link with the Community * * *. That principle must be deemed to extend also to cases in which there is a sufficiently close link between the employment relationship, on the one hand, and the law of a Member State and thus the relevant rules of Community law, on the other.

16. In the present case, it is clear from the documents before the Court that the plaintiff's situation is subject to rules of German law in several respects. First, her contract of employment was entered into in accordance with the law of the Member State which

employs her and it is only pursuant to that law that it was stipulated that her conditions of employment were to be determined in accordance with Algerian law. Secondly, that contract contains a clause giving jurisdiction over any dispute between the parties concerning the contract to the courts in Bonn and, ultimately, Berlin. Thirdly, the plaintiff in the main proceedings is affiliated for pension purposes to the German State social security system and is subject, though to a limited extent, to German income tax.

17. In situations such as that of the plaintiff in the main proceedings, Community law and thus the prohibition of discrimination based on nationality contained in the abovementioned Community provisions are applicable to all aspects of the employment relationship which are governed by the law of a Member State.

18. The German Government maintains, however, that Ms Boukhalfa's conditions of employment are governed by Algerian law and that the abovementioned Community provisions prohibiting discrimination based on nationality are therefore inapplicable.

19. As has been pointed out in paragraph 16 above, however, it is only pursuant to Paragraph 33 of the [German Law on the Diplomatic Service] that Algerian law determines Ms Boukhalfa's conditions of employment and it is the compatibility of that paragraph with Community law which is in issue in the main proceedings.

20. The German Government further objects that, even before the contract was entered into, the plaintiff in the main proceedings was resident not in one of the Member States but in Algeria. The national court points out, moreover, that the contract of employment was entered into and is permanently performed in Algeria.

21. Those circumstances are not, however, such as to call into question the links with Community law noted above.

22. The answer to the national court' s question must therefore be that the prohibition of discrimination based on nationality, laid down in Article 48 (2) of the Treaty and Article 7(1) and (4) of Regulation No 1612/68, applies to a national of a Member State who is permanently resident in a non-member country, who is employed by another Member State in its embassy in that non-member country and whose contract of employment was entered into and is permanently performed there, as regards all aspects of the employment relationship which are governed by the legislation of the employing Member State.

Notes and Questions

1. **Open Issues?** Would the rationale of *Boukhalfa* apply to other forms of discrimination forbidden by the EU, such as sex, race, disabili-

ty discrimination? Would it apply to private discrimination by a German employer against a Belgian national in Algeria? Are EU and American employment discrimination rules similar or different with respect to extraterritorial application?

2. **Extraterritorial Application of U.K. Discrimination Law?** The employment discrimination law of Great Britain does not apply generally outside the its territory. For example, section 6 of the Sex Discrimination Act 1975, as amended, provides: "It is unlawful for a person, in relation to employment by him at an establishment in" Great Britain, to discriminate [based on sex]...." Thus, a British employer in the United States is not subject to British fair employment law respecting its activities in the U.S. Similarly, the preamble to European Union Directive 2000/78 declares that discrimination based on religion or belief, disability, age or sexual orientation [in employment and specified other activities] "should be prohibited throughout the Community," but does not mention employment outside its territory.

However, in three consolidated British wrongful-discharge, but not discrimination, cases, the House of Lords panel applied conflict of laws principles to decide whether the (U.K.) Employment Rights Act 1996 applied to employment outside Great Britian.

LAWSON v SERCO LTD.

[2006] UKHL 3, 1 All ER 823 (H.L.)

[Eds. The appeal involved three consolidated unfair dismissal cases: (1) In Lawson v. Serco, the plaintiff worked as a security supervisor for a U.K. company on Ascension Island, a dependency of the British Overseas Territory of St. Helena. After six months on the island, Mr. Lawson resigned, claiming that he had been constructively dismissed. (2) In Botham v. Ministry of Defence, the plaintiff was a youth worker at various U.K. Ministry of Defence establishments in Germany. In accordance with the NATO Status of Forces Agreement of 1951 he was part of the "civil component" of the British forces in Germany and treated as resident in the U.K. rather than Germany for various purposes including taxation. In September 2003 he was summarily dismissed on allegations of gross misconduct but claims that his dismissal was unfair. (3) In Crofts v. Veta, Ltd., the plaintiff was based at Heathrow so that he could live in the U.K. but worked for a wholly owned subsidiary of Cathay Pacific Airways, both Hong Kong companies. In July 2001, he was dismissed in circumstances which he claims were unfair. The lead speech, i.e., opinion by Lord Hoffmann states in part:]

* * *

1. My Lords, the question common to these three appeals is the territorial scope of section 94(1) of the Employment Rights Act

1996, which gives employees the right not to be unfairly dismissed. Section 230(1) of the 1996 Act defines an "employee" as an individual "who has entered into or works under (or, where the employment has ceased, worked under) a contract of employment". But the Act contains no geographic limitation. Read literally, it applies to any individual who works under a contract of employment anywhere in the world. It is true that section 244(1) says that the 1996 Act "extends" to England and Wales and Scotland ('Great Britain'). But that means only that it forms part of the law of Great Britain and does not form part of the law of any other territory (like Northern Ireland or the Channel Islands) for which Parliament could have legislated. It tells us nothing about the connection, if any, which an employee or his employment must have with Great Britain. Nevertheless, all parties to these appeals are agreed that some territorial limitations must be implied. It is inconceivable that Parliament was intending to confer rights upon employees working in foreign countries and having no connection with Great Britain. The argument has been over what those limitations should be. Putting the question in the traditional terms of the conflict of laws, what connection between Great Britain and the employment relationship is required to make section 94(1) the appropriate choice of law in deciding whether and in what circumstances an employee can complain that his dismissal was unfair? * * *.

20. Mr. Lawson's case against Serco Ltd was in many respects similar to that of Mr. Botham: both had been recruited in Great Britain to work abroad. * * *

21. The issues in the Crofts case were rather different. While Lawson and Botham might be called expatriate employees, working abroad in circumstances in which their work nevertheless had strong connections with Great Britain, Mr Crofts was perhaps an extreme example of a peripatetic employee, whose work constantly took him to many different places. * * *

PERIPATETIC EMPLOYEES

28. As Crofts v. Veta Ltd shows, the concept of employment in Great Britain may not be easy to apply to peripatetic employees. * * *

29. I think that we are today more concerned with how the contract was in fact being operated at the time of the dismissal than with the terms of the original contract. But the common sense of treating the base of a peripatetic employee as, for the purposes of the statute, his place of employment, remains valid. It was applied by the Court of Appeal to an airline pilot in Todd v. British Midland Airways Ltd[,] [1978] ICR 959 at 964, where Lord Denning MR said:

> "A man's base is the place where he should be regarded as ordinarily working, even though he may spend days, weeks or months working overseas. I would only make this suggestion. I do not think that the terms of the contract help much in these cases. As a rule, there is no term in the contract about exactly where he is to work. You have to go by the conduct of the parties and the way they have been operating the contract. You have to find at the material time where the man is based."

* * *

The employment tribunal made certain 'primary findings of fact' (at para [5]):

> "(6) In the early 1990s, largely for economic reasons [Cathay Pacific] entered into negotiations with the trade union representing their aircrew with a view to formulating a "basings policy" designed to enable aircrew to live in, and work from, other parts of the world. Negotiations were successful and a "Basings Agreement" was concluded. The agreement provided that a new company would be set up to employ those aircrew who had volunteered for, and been granted, a foreign basing . . .
>
> (8) The basings policy embodied and/or was operated on (among others) the following principles:
>
> > (a) [Cathay Pacific] aircrew who applied successfully for a basing outside Hong Kong would be required to resign their employment with [Cathay] and transfer to the employment of a subsidiary company of [Cathay] (Veta).
> >
> > (b) any pilot transferred to a new basing would be allocated a "home base" from which his . . . flying cycles would ordinarily commence and at which they would ordinarily commence and . . . end.
> >
> > (c) There was no express requirement for aircrew to reside close to their home base or even within the relevant base area. On the other hand, staff rostered for reserve duty were required to be within two hours travel of their home base for the periods to which that rostered duty related.
> >
> > (d) Unlike expatriate aircrew living in Hong Kong, those transferring to new bases would not be eligible for financial support in respect of living accommodation and other expenses.
> >
> > (e) Transferring employees would be responsible for their own taxation and immigration arrangements."

33. Having considered these and other facts, such as the way in which the Veta pilots were managed from Hong Kong, the Tribunal reached the following conclusion:

> "Pursuant to the basings policy the Veta applicants were required to resign their [Cathay] employment and did so irrevocably. They were allocated new bases on the footing that they would remain their indefinitely. They were repatriated from Hong Kong and ceased to be resident there. Their tours of duty began and ended in London. Even if a flying cycle began elsewhere, the tour of duty began when they reported to London Heathrow for the purpose of being 'positioned' to the port from which the flying cycle was to commence. They were paid a salary designed to reflect a lower cost of living than that experienced in Hong Kong. In short, the centre of their operations was, quite manifestly, London."

* * *

34. * * * In the present case I think not only that the tribunal was entitled to reach the conclusion which it did but also that it was right. I would therefore dismiss Veta's appeal.

EXPATRIATE EMPLOYEES

35. The problem of what I might call the expatriate employees is rather more difficult. The concept of a base, which is useful to locate the workplace of a peripatetic employee, provides no help in the case of an expatriate employee. The Ministry of Defence accepts that Mr. Botham fell within the scope of section 94(1), but his base was the base and the base was in Germany.

36. The circumstances would have to be unusual for an employee who works and is based abroad to come within the scope of British labour legislation. But I think that there are some who do. I hesitate to describe such cases as coming within an exception or exceptions to the general rule because that suggests a definition more precise than can be imposed upon the many possible combinations of factors, some of which may be unforeseen. * * *

37. First, I think that it would be very unlikely that someone working abroad would be within the scope of section 94(1) unless he was working for an employer based in Great Britain. But that would not be enough. Many companies based in Great Britain also carry on business in other countries and employment in those businesses will not attract British law merely on account of British ownership. The fact that the employee also happens to be British or even that he was recruited in Britain, so that the relationship was "rooted and forged" in this country, should not in itself be sufficient to take the case out of the general rule that the place of employment is decisive. Something more is necessary.

38. Something more may be provided by the fact that the employee is posted abroad by a British employer for the purposes of a business carried on in Great Britain. He is not working for a business conducted in a foreign country which belongs to British owners or is a branch of a British business, but as representative of a business conducted at home. I have in mind, for example, a foreign correspondent on the staff of a British newspaper, who is posted to Rome or Peking and may remain for years living in Italy or China but remains nevertheless a permanent employee of the newspaper who could be posted to some other country. He would in my opinion fall within the scope of section 94(1). * * *

39. Another example is an expatriate employee of a British employer who is operating within what amounts for practical purposes to an extra-territorial British enclave in a foreign country. This was the position of Mr. Botham working in a military base in Germany. And I think, although the case is not quite so strong, that the same is true of Mr. Lawson at the RAF base on Ascension Island. While it is true that Mr. Lawson was there in a support role, employed by a private firm to provide security on the base, I think it would be unrealistic to regard him as having taken up employment in a foreign community in the same way as if Serco Ltd were providing security services for a hospital in Berlin. I have no doubt that Bryant v. Foreign and Commonwealth Office[,] [2003] All ER (D) 104 (May), in which it was held that section 94(1) did not apply to a British national locally engaged to work in the British Embassy in Rome, was rightly decided. But on Ascension there was no local community. In practice, as opposed to constitutional theory, the base was a British outpost in the South Atlantic. Although there was a local system of law, the connection between the employment relationship and the United Kingdom were overwhelmingly stronger. * * *

41. Finally I should note that in the case of expatriate employees, it is quite possible that they will be entitled to make claims under both the local law and section 94(1). For example, the foreign correspondent living in Rome would be entitled to rights in Italian law under the Posted Workers Directive and although the Directive does not extend to claims for unfair dismissal, Italian domestic law may nevertheless provide for them. Obviously there cannot be double recovery and any compensation paid under the foreign system would have to be taken into account by an employment tribunal.

Notes and Questions

1. **1999 Amendment to U.K. Sex Discrimination Law**. It would appear that U.K. discrimination law may have some extraterrito-

rial reach in view of 1999 amendments to the Sex Discrimination Act of 1975, section 10 of which now provides that:

> (1) For purposes of this Part and [section] 1 of the Equal Pay Act of 1970 * * *, employment is to be regarded as being at an establishment in Great Britain [if]—
>
> (a) the employee does his work wholly or partly in Great Britain, or
>
> (b) the employee does his work wholly outside Great Britain and subsection 1(A) applies.
>
> 1(A) This subsection applies if—
>
> (a) the employer has a place of business at an establishment in Great Britain,
>
> (b) the work is for the purpose of the business carried on at that establishment, and
>
> (c) the employee is ordinarily resident in Great Britain—
>
> (i) at the time when he applies for or is offered the employment, or
>
> (ii) at any time during the course of the employment.

Consider how this statute would be applied in the case of the foreign correspondent of a U.K. newspaper discussed in Lord Hoffman's opinion.

2. **Rome Convention**. Consider also the Rome Convention, which is part of the U.K. Contracts (Applicable Law) Act of 1990:

> Article 3. Freedom of choice
>
> 1. A contract shall be governed by the law chosen by the parties. The choice must be express or demonstrated with reasonable certainty by the terms of the contract or the circumstances of the case. By their choice the parties can select the law applicable to the whole or a part only of the contract.
>
> 2. The parties may at any time agree to subject the contract to a law other than that which previously governed it, whether as a result of an earlier choice under this Article or of other provisions of this Convention. Any variation by the parties of the law to be applied made after the conclusion of the contract shall not prejudice its formal validity under Article 9 or adversely affect the rights of third parties.
>
> 3. The fact that the parties have chosen a foreign law, whether or not accompanied by the choice of a foreign tribunal, shall not, where all the other elements relevant to the situation at the time of the choice are connected with one country only, prejudice the application of rules of the law of that country which cannot be derogated from by contract, hereinafter called "mandatory rules".

4. The existence and validity of the consent of the parties as to the choice of the applicable law shall be determined in accordance with the provisions of Articles 8, 9 and 11.

Article 4. Applicable law in the absence of choice

1. To the extent that the law applicable to the contract has not been chosen in accordance with Article 3, the contract shall be governed by the law of the country with which it is most closely connected. Nevertheless, a severable part of the contract which has a closer connection with another country may by way of exception be governed by the law of that other country.

2. Subject to the provisions of paragraph 5 of this Article, it shall be presumed that the contract is most closely connected with the country where the party who is to effect the performance which is characteristic of the contract has, at the time of conclusion of the contract, his habitual residence, or, in the case of a body corporate or unincorporate, its central administration. However, if the contract is entered into in the course of that party's trade or profession, that country shall be the country in which the principal place of business is situated or, where under the terms of the contract the performance is to be effected through a place of business other than the principal place of business, the country in which that other place of business is situated.

* * *

5. Paragraph 2 shall not apply if the characteristic performance cannot be determined, and the presumptions in paragraphs 2, 3 and 4 shall be disregarded if it appears from the circumstances as a whole that the contract is more closely connected with another country.

* * *

Article 6. Individual employment contracts

1. Notwithstanding the provisions of Article 3, in a contract of employment a choice of law made by the parties shall not have the result of depriving the employee of the protection afforded to him by the mandatory rules of the law which would be applicable under paragraph 2 in the absence of choice.

2. Notwithstanding the provisions of Article 4, a contract of employment shall, in the absence of choice in accordance with Article 3, be governed:

(a) by the law of the country in which the employee habitually carries out his work in performance of the contract, even if he is temporarily employed in another country; or

(b) if the employee does not habitually carry out his work in any one country, by the law of the country in which the place of business through which he was engaged is situated;

unless it appears from the circumstances as a whole that the contract is more closely connected with another country, in which case the contract shall be governed by the law of that country.

Article 7. Mandatory rules

1. When applying under this Convention the law of a country, effect may be given to the mandatory rules of the law of another country with which the situation has a close connection, if and in so far as, under the law of the latter country, those rules must be applied whatever the law applicable to the contract. In considering whether to give effect to these mandatory rules, regard shall be had to their nature and purpose and to the consequences of their application or non-application.

2. Nothing in this Convention shall restrict the application of the rules of the law of the forum in a situation where they are mandatory irrespective of the law otherwise applicable to the contract.

Chapter Two

PROTECTED CLASSES

In the United States, the scope of fair employment law has gradually expanded. A Reconstruction statute, 42 U.S.C. § 1981, forbids race discrimination in employment. The first anti-discrimination law in the modern era, the Equal Pay Act of 1963, 29 U.S.C. § 206(d), required employers to pay men and women receive equal pay for equal work. Title VII of the Civil Rights Act of 1964, 42 U.S.C. § 2000e, bans employment discrimination based on race, color, religion, sex, or national origin. The Age Discrimination in Employment Act of 1967, 29 U.S.C. § 621 et seq., protects workers over the age of 40 from age bias. The Immigration Reform and Control Act of 1986, 8 U.S.C. § 1324b, forbids citizenship-based discrimination against aliens who are lawfully working in the U.S. And the Americans with Disabilities Act of 1990, 42 U.S.C. § 12111, et seq., bars discrimination against the disabled. Federal law to date has not banned discrimination based on sexual orientation, although several state and local governments have done so. Nor does federal law directly address discrimination based on tribe or caste. Race was the paradigm for anti-discrimination legislation in the U.S. The materials in this chapter show the influence of U.S. law on choices other countries have made to protect various classes from employment discrimination.

A. EUROPEAN REGULATION

1. Expanding the Reach of the Ban on Sex Discrimination

The 1957 treaty establishing the European Union's predecessor, the European Community, provided in Article 119:

> Each Member State shall ensure that the principle of equal pay for male and female workers for equal work or work of equal value is applied.

The European Court of Justice (the highest court of the EU) held that Article 119, standing alone, did not guarantee "the observance of the principle of equality between men and women in working conditions other than remuneration." *Defrenne v. Sabena*, [1978] ECR 1365. Despite the express terms of Article 119, the Council of the European Community (one of the EU's law-making bodies) had earlier adopted Directive 76/207/EEC, which also required "equal treatment for men and women" in access to employment and in conditions of employment. By 1997, in the Treaty of Amsterdam, Article 119 [now 141] endorsed Directive 76/207:

> The Council . . . shall adopt measures to ensure the application of the principle of equal opportunities and equal treatment of men and women in matters of employment and occupation, including the principle of equal pay for equal work or work of equal value.

Thus, the EU from the outset forbade sex-based pay discrimination and then expanded protection, by banning sex discrimination in employment. While also forbidding "discrimination based on nationality between workers of the Member States" in employment, the 1957 treaty did not reach discrimination based on race, religion, disability, national origin, sexual orientation or age. European nations had also adopted the European Convention on Human Rights in 1953. Article 14 of the Convention banned "discrimination on any ground such as sex, race, colour, language, religion, political or other opinion, national or social origin, association with a national minority, property, birth or other status," but the ban applied only to "the enjoyment of the rights and freedoms set forth in this Convention." Employment was not mentioned as a protected right. However, the European Court of Human Rights (ECHR), which sits to adjudicate violations of the Convention, later found that granting parental leave to women employees but not to men constituted forbidden sex discrimination that violated the Convention. Article 8 of the Convention creates a right to respect for family life. The Court linked Article 14's discrimination ban with Article 8, saying:

> The aid here in question, namely parental leave payments, is nevertheless destined to promote family life. The notion of discrimination comprises in general cases where a person or group is treated, without proper justification, less favourably than another, even though the more favourable treatment is not called for by the Convention. Therefore the facts at issue fall within the ambit of Article 8.

A.P. v. Austria, 20 Eur. H. Rep. CD 63 (1995).

ELISABETH JOHANNA PACIFICA DEKKER v STICHTING VORMINGSCENTRUM VOOR JONG VOLWASSENEN (VJV–CENTRUM) PLUS

[1990] ECR I–3941

[Eds. This decision addressed the question whether refusal to employ a woman because she is pregnant constitutes sex discrimination under Council Directive 76/207.]

9. Article 2(1) of the Directive provides that "... the principle of equal treatment shall mean that there shall be no discrimination whatsoever on grounds of sex either directly or indirectly by reference in particular to marital or family status". Under Article 3(1) "application of the principle of equal treatment means that there shall be no discrimination whatsoever on grounds of sex in the conditions, including selection criteria, for access to all jobs or posts ...".

* * *

11. The reason given by the employer for refusing to appoint Mrs. Dekker is basically that it could not have obtained reimbursement from the Risicofonds [Assurance Fund for the provision of social benefits in special education] benefits which it would have had to pay her for the duration of her absence due to pregnancy, and yet at the same time it would have been obliged to employ a replacement. That situation arises because, on the one hand, the national scheme in question assimilates pregnancy to sickness and, on the other, [the insurer's internal rules governing daily sickness benefits] contain[ ] no provision excluding pregnancy from the cases in which the Risicofonds is entitled to refuse reimbursement of the daily benefits.

12. In that regard it should be observed that only women can be refused employment on grounds of pregnancy and such a refusal therefore constitutes direct discrimination on grounds of sex. A refusal of employment on account of the financial consequences of absence due to pregnancy must be regarded as based, essentially, on the fact of pregnancy. Such discrimination cannot be justified on grounds relating to the financial loss which an employer who appointed a pregnant woman would suffer for the duration of her maternity leave.

* * *

14. It follows from the foregoing that the answer to be given to the first question is that an employer is in direct contravention of the principle of equal treatment embodied in Articles 2(1) and 3(1) of Council Directive 76/207 of 9 February 1976 on the imple-

mentation of the principle of equal treatment for men and women as regards access to employment, vocational training and promotion, and working conditions if he refuses to enter into a contract of employment with a female candidate whom he considers to be suitable for the job where such refusal is based on the possible adverse consequences for him of employing a pregnant woman, owing to rules on unfitness for work adopted by the public authorities which assimilate inability to work on account of pregnancy and confinement to inability to work on account of illness.

P v S AND CORNWALL COUNTY COUNCIL

[1996] ECR I–2143

12. A dismissal, such as is in issue in the main proceedings, must be considered in the light of Article 5(1) of the Directive [76/2007/EEC], which provides that:

> "Application of the principle of equal treatment with regard to working conditions, including the conditions governing dismissal, means that men and women shall be guaranteed the same conditions without discrimination on grounds of sex."

13. The industrial tribunal's two questions, which may appropriately be considered together, must therefore be construed as asking whether, having regard to the purpose of the Directive, Article 5(1) precludes dismissal of a transsexual for a reason related to his or her gender reassignment.

* * *

15. [T]he United Kingdom points out in particular that it appears from the order for reference that the employer would also have dismissed P. if P. had previously been a woman and had undergone an operation to become a man.

16. The European Court of Human Rights has held that "the term 'transsexual' is usually applied to those who, whilst belonging physically to one sex, feel convinced that they belong to the other; that they often seek to achieve a more integrated, unambiguous identity by undergoing medical treatment and surgical operations to adapt their physical characteristics to their psychological nature. Transsexuals who have been operated upon thus form a fairly well-defined and identifiable group."

17. The principle of equal treatment "for men and women" to which the Directive refers in its title, preamble and provisions means, as Articles 2(1) and 3(1) in particular indicate, that there should be "no discrimination whatsoever on grounds of sex".

18. Thus the Directive is simply the expression, in the relevant field, of the principle of equality, which is one of the fundamental principles of Community law.

* * *

20. Accordingly, the scope of the Directive cannot be confined simply to discrimination based on the fact that a person is of one sex or the other sex. In view of its purpose and the nature of the rights which it seeks to safeguard, the scope of the Directive is also to apply to discrimination arising, as in this case, from the gender reassignment of the person concerned.

21. Such discrimination is based, essentially if not exclusively, on the sex of the person concerned. Where such a person is dismissed on the ground that he or she intends to undergo, or has undergone, gender reassignment, he or she is treated unfavourably by comparison with persons of the sex to which he or she was deemed to belong before undergoing gender reassignment.

22. To tolerate such discrimination would be tantamount, as regards such a person, to a failure to respect the dignity and freedom to which he or she is entitled, and which the Court has a duty to safeguard.

23. Dismissal of such a person must therefore be regarded as contrary to article 5(1) of the Directive, unless the dismissal could be justified under Article 2(2). There is, however, no material before the court to suggest that this was so here.

Notes and Questions

1. **Why the Equal Pay Issue Came First?** The European Union began as an economic entity, a common market. What prompted it to require equal pay for men and women? Why did it not initially bar other forms of employment discrimination as well? One author explains:

> Although the EEC was fundamentally conceived as an economic rather than a political entity, France, which itself already had an equal pay law, successfully argued that it would be placed at an unfair competitive disadvantage if other Member States were permitted to pay women less for the same work.

Sandra Fredman, Discrimination Law, 31–32 (2002). Almost twenty years after the Treaty of Rome created the EEC, the European Court of Justice gave an additional reason for Article 119:

> First, in the light of the different stages of the development of social legislation in the various Member States, the aim of Article 119 is to avoid a situation in which undertakings established in states which have actually implemented the principle of equal pay suffer a competitive disadvantage in intra-Community competition

as compared with undertakings established in states which have not yet eliminated discrimination against women workers as regards pay.

Secondly, this provision forms part of the social objectives of the Community, which is not merely an economic union, but is at the same time intended, by common action, to ensure social progress and seek the constant improvement of the living and working conditions of their peoples, as is emphasized by the preamble to the Treaty.

Gabrielle Defrenne v. Societe Anonyme Belge de Navigation Aerienne Sabena, [1976] ECR 455. Would this reasoning also suggest banning discrimination based on race, religion, national origin, disability, age?

2. **Does "Sex" Discrimination Include "Same Sex" Discrimination?** In spite of the ruling in *P v. S and Cornwall County Council*, two years later the European Court of Justice held that the refusal by an employer to give free train tickets to the person of the same sex with whom a worker has a stable relationship, where it would give free tickets "to a worker's spouse or to the person of the opposite sex with whom a worker has a stable relationship outside marriage, does not constitute [sex] discrimination. . . ." Lisa Jacqueline Grant v South–West Trains Ltd., [1998] ECR I–621, 653. The Court seemingly accepted an argument that it had rejected in the *Cornwall County Council* case, reasoning "Since the condition imposed by the undertaking's regulations applies in the same way to female and male workers, it cannot be regarded as constituting discrimination directly based on sex." Id. at 646.

The EU in Directive 2000/78 made clear (in Articles 1–2) that sexual orientation was included among the prohibited acts of discrimination and that member states would be obligated to enact implementing legislation.

3. **Treatment of Pregnancy–Based Discrimination.** Does the prohibition of sex discrimination necessarily include pregnancy-based discrimination? Compare the reasoning in *Dekker* with the U.S. Supreme Court's decision in General Electric Corp. v. Gilbert, 429 U.S. 125 (1976). Is the decision in *Grant* (discrimination based on sex of partner is not sex discrimination) compatible with *Cornwall County* (discrimination based on gender transformation is sex discrimination)? How would U.S. courts decide these cases? Note that two years after the decision in *Dekker*, the Commission adopted Directive 92/85, which treats pregnancy as a health and safety issue:

COUNCIL DIRECTIVE 92/85/EEC

1992 O.J. (L 348) 1 (EC)

Article 10

Prohibition of dismissal

In order to guarantee workers, within the meaning of Article 2, the exercise of their health and safety protection rights as recognized under this Article, it shall be provided that:

1. Member States shall take the necessary measures to prohibit the dismissal of workers, within the meaning of Article 2, during the period from the beginning of their pregnancy to the end of the maternity leave referred to in Article 8 (1), save in exceptional cases not connected with their condition which are permitted under national legislation and/or practice and, where applicable, provided that the competent authority has given its consent;

2. if a worker, within the meaning of Article 2, is dismissed during the period referred to in point 1, the employer must cite duly substantiated grounds for her dismissal in writing;

3. Member States shall take the necessary measures to protect workers, within the meaning of Article 2, from consequences of dismissal which is unlawful by virtue of point 1.

Article 11

Employment rights

In order to guarantee workers within the meaning of Article 2 the exercise of their health and safety protection rights as recognised in this Article, it shall be provided that:

1. in the cases referred to in Articles 5, 6 and 7, the employment rights relating to the employment contract, including the maintenance of a payment to, and/or entitlement to an adequate allowance for, workers within the meaning of Article 2, must be ensured in accordance with national legislation and/or national practice;

2. in the case referred to in Article 8, the following must be ensured:

   (a) the rights connected with the employment contract of workers within the meaning of Article 2, other than those referred to in point (b) below;

   (b) maintenance of a payment to, and/or entitlement to an adequate allowance for, workers within the meaning of Article 2;

3. the allowance referred to in point 2 (b) shall be deemed adequate if it guarantees income at least equivalent to that which the worker concerned would receive in the event of a break in her activities on grounds connected with her state of health, subject to any ceiling laid down under national legislation;

4. Member States may make entitlement to pay or the allowance referred to in points 1 and 2 (b) conditional upon the worker concerned fulfilling the conditions of eligibility for such benefits laid down under national legislation.

These conditions may under no circumstances provide for periods of previous employment in excess of 12 months immediately prior to the presumed date of confinement.

Is the EU's approach under the banner of health-safety regulation preferable to use of the anti-discrimination laws? Consider Evelyn Ellis, EU Antidiscrimination Law 241 (2005): "In so far as this [Directive] attempts to create a special legal regime to deal with the rights of pregnant workers, it is to be welcomed; in the view of the present writer ... since pregnancy and childbirth are situations which are unique to women, it is inappropriate to use the anti-discrimination legislation as the chief legal vehicle to cater for them. It is certainly vital to the concept of substantive equality for special rules to exist to cater for maternity rights for workers, but such rules need to be additional to the normal non-discrimination principle."

4. **Treatment of Fetal Harm Issues?** Is it a violation of the anti-discrimination laws for an employer to bar female employees still capable of childbirth from jobs that pose a risk of fetal harm? Recall the U.S. Supreme Court's decision in UAW v. Johnson Controls, Inc., 499 U.S. 187 (1991). Compare Directive 92/85 on these issues:

COUNCIL DIRECTIVE 92/85/EEC

1992 O.J. (L 348) 1 (EC)

Article 5

1. Without prejudice to Article 6 of Directive 89/391/EEC, if the results of the assessment referred to in Article 4 (1) reveal a risk to the safety or health or an effect on the pregnancy or breastfeeding of a worker within the meaning of Article 2, the employer shall take the necessary measures to ensure that, by temporarily adjusting the working conditions and/or the working hours of the worker concerned, the exposure of that worker to such risks is avoided.

2. If the adjustment of her working conditions and/or working hours is not technically and/or objectively feasible, or cannot reasonably be required on duly substantiated grounds, the employ-

er shall take the necessary measures to move the worker concerned to another job.

3. If moving her to another job is not technically and/or objectively feasible or cannot reasonably be required on duly substantiated grounds, the worker concerned shall be granted leave in accordance with national legislation and/or national practice for the whole of the period necessary to protect her safety or health * * *.

Article 6

In addition to the general provisions concerning the protection of workers, in particular those relating to the limit values for occupational exposure:

1. Pregnant workers within the meaning of Article 2 (a) may under no circumstances be obliged to perform duties for which the assessment has revealed a risk of exposure, which would jeopardise safety or health, to the agents and working conditions listed in Annex II, Section A;

2. Workers who are breastfeeding, within the meaning of Article 2 (c), may under no circumstances be obliged to perform duties for which the assessment has revealed a risk of exposure, which would jeopardise safety or health, to the agents and working conditions listed in Annex II, Section B.

2. EU's 2000 Directives: Examples of Disability and Age Discrimination

In 2000 the EU adopted two Directives which create "a framework for combating discrimination on the grounds of racial or ethnic origin, with a view to putting into effect in the Member States the principle of equal treatment," Council Directive 2000/43, 2000 O.J. (L 180) 22 (EC); and "a general framework for combating discrimination on the grounds of religion or belief, disability, age or sexual orientation as regards employment and occupation" 2000/78 (excerpted below). These two directives dramatically enlarge the scope of the EU's fair employment laws. We focus below on the latter directive.

COUNCIL DIRECTIVE 2000/78/EC

2000 O.J. (L 303) 16 (EC)

Article 1

Purpose

The purpose of this Directive is to lay down a general framework for combating discrimination on the grounds of religion or belief, disability, age or sexual orientation as regards employment and occupation, with a view to putting into effect in the Member States the principle of equal treatment.

ARTICLE 2

Concept of discrimination

1.

For the purposes of this Directive, the 'principle of equal treatment' shall mean that there shall be no direct or indirect discrimination whatsoever on any of the grounds referred to in Article 1.

2.

For the purposes of paragraph 1:

(a) direct discrimination shall be taken to occur where one person is treated less favourably than another is, has been or would be treated in a comparable situation, on any of the grounds referred to in Article 1;

(b) indirect discrimination shall be taken to occur where an apparently neutral provision, criterion or practice would put persons having a particular religion or belief, a particular disability, a particular age, or a particular sexual orientation at a particular disadvantage compared with other persons unless: (i) that provision, criterion or practice is objectively justified by a legitimate aim and the means of achieving that aim are appropriate and necessary, or (ii) as regards persons with a particular disability, the employer or any person or organisation to whom this Directive applies, is obliged, under national legislation, to take appropriate measures in line with the principles contained in Article 5 in order to eliminate disadvantages entailed by such provision, criterion or practice.

ARTICLE 3

Harassment shall be deemed to be a form of discrimination within the meaning of paragraph 1, when unwanted conduct related to any of the grounds referred to in Article 1 takes place with the purpose or effect of violating the dignity of a person and of creating an intimidating, hostile, degrading, humiliating or offensive environment. In this context, the concept of harassment may be defined in accordance with the national laws and practice of the Member States.

* * *

ARTICLE 5

Reasonable accommodation for disabled persons

In order to guarantee compliance with the principle of equal treatment in relation to persons with disabilities, reasonable accommodation shall be provided. This means that employers shall take appropriate measures, where needed in a particular case, to enable a person with a disability to have access to, participate in, or advance in employment, or to undergo training, unless such measures would impose a disproportionate burden on the employer. This burden shall not be disproportionate when it is sufficiently remedied by measures existing within the framework of the disability policy of the Member State concerned.

Article 6

Justification of differences of treatment on grounds of age

1.

Notwithstanding Article 2(2), Member States may provide that differences of treatment on grounds of age shall not constitute discrimination, if, within the context of national law,they are objectively and reasonably justified by a legitimate aim, including legitimate employment policy, labour market and vocational training objectives, and if the means of achieving that aim are appropriate and necessary. Such differences of treatment may include, among others: (a) the setting of special conditions on access to employment and vocational training, employment and occupation, including dismissal and remuneration conditions, for young people, older workers and persons with caring responsibilities in order to promote their vocational integration or ensure their protection; (b) the fixing of minimum conditions of age, professional experience or seniority in service for access to employment or to certain advantages linked to employment;(c) the fixing of a maximum age for recruitment which is based on the training requirements of the post in question or the need for a reasonable period of employment before retirement.

2.

Notwithstanding Article 2(2), Member States may provide that the fixing for occupational social security schemes of ages for admission or entitlement to retirement or invalidity benefits, including the fixing under those schemes of different ages for employees or groups or categories of employees, and the use, in the context of such schemes, of age criteria in actuarial calculations, does not constitute discrimination on the grounds of age, provided this does not result in discrimination on the grounds of sex.

Article 7

Positive action

1.

With a view to ensuring full equality in practice, the principle of equal treatment shall not prevent any Member State from maintaining or adopting specific measures to prevent or compensate for disadvantages linked to any of the grounds referred to in Article 1.

2.

With regard to disabled persons, the principle of equal treatment shall be without prejudice to the right of Member States to maintain or adopt provisions on the protection of health and safety at work or to measures aimed at creating or maintaining provisions or facilities for safeguarding or promoting their integration into the working environment.

ARTICLE 8

Minimum requirements

1.

Member States may introduce or maintain provisions which are more favourable to the protection of the principle of equal treatment than those laid down in this Directive.

2.

The implementation of this Directive shall under no circumstances constitute grounds for a reduction in the level of protection against discrimination already afforded by Member States in the fields covered by this Directive.

Notes and Questions

1. **Relevance of Original Rationale?** Does the original rationale for adopting the equal pay article of the Treaty of Rome also explain the reach of the 2000 Directives?

2. **"Indirect" Discrimination.** Note the introduction of the concept of "indirect" discrimination in both directives. How, if at all, is the formulation different from the concept of "disparate impact" under Title VII? See also pp. 93–99 infra.

3. **Treatment of Age Bias**. How, if at all, are the provisions on disability and age bias different from U.S. law? Is age-based mandatory retirement now unlawful under EU law?

4. **Absenteeism as a Disability?** Is absenteeism due to illness a form of disability? This is the subject of the opinion that follows.

SONIA CHACÓN NAVAS v EUREST COLECTIVIDADES SA

[2006] ECR I–6467

[Eds. This case considers whether sickness is a "disability" under Directive 2000/78. Chacón Navas was fired from her job for absenteeism due to illness.]

39. The concept of "disability" is not defined by Directive 2000/78 itself. Nor does the directive refer to the laws of the Member States for the definition of that concept. * * *

43. Directive 2000/78 aims to combat certain types of discrimination as regards employment and occupation. In that context, the concept of "disability" must be understood as referring to a limitation which results in particular from physical, mental or psychological impairments and which hinders the participation of the person concerned in professional life.

44. However, by using the concept of "disability" in Article 1 of that directive, the legislature deliberately chose a term which differs from "sickness". The two concepts cannot therefore simply be treated as being the same.

45. Recital 16 in the preamble to Directive 2000/78 states that the "provision of measures to accommodate the needs of disabled people at the workplace plays an important role in combating discrimination on grounds of disability". The importance which the Community legislature attaches to measures for adapting the workplace to the disability demonstrates that it envisaged situations in which participation in professional life is hindered over a long period of time. In order for the limitation to fall within the concept of "disability", it must therefore be probable that it will last for a long time.

46. There is nothing in Directive 2000/78 to suggest that workers are protected by the prohibition of discrimination on grounds of disability as soon as they develop any type of sickness.

47. It follows from the above considerations that a person who has been dismissed by his employer solely on account of sickness does not fall within the general framework laid down for combating discrimination on grounds of disability by Directive 2000/78 * * *.

49. According to Recital 17 in the preamble to Directive 2000/78, that directive does not require the recruitment, promotion or maintenance in employment of an individual who is not competent, capable and available to perform the essential functions of the

post concerned, without prejudice to the obligation to provide reasonable accommodation for people with disabilities.

* * *

52. It follows from all the above considerations that the answer to the first question must be that:

— a person who has been dismissed by his employer solely on account of sickness does not fall within the general framework laid down for combating discrimination on grounds of disability by Directive 2000/78;

— the prohibition, as regards dismissal, of discrimination on grounds of disability contained in Articles 2(1) and 3(1)(c) of Directive 2000/78 precludes dismissal on grounds of disability which, in the light of the obligation to provide reasonable accommodation for people with disabilities, is not justified by the fact that the person concerned is not competent, capable and available to perform the essential functions of his post.

53. By its second question, the referring court is asking whether sickness can be regarded as a ground in addition to those in relation to which Directive 2000/78 prohibits discrimination.

54. In this connection, it must be stated that no provision of the EC Treaty prohibits discrimination on grounds of sickness as such.

55. * * * Article 13 EC does not refer to discrimination on grounds of sickness as such in addition to discrimination on grounds of disability, and cannot therefore even constitute a legal basis for Council measures to combat such discrimination.

B. GREAT BRITAIN

Great Britain's first law against race discrimination, the Race Relations Act 1965, did not apply to employment. Three years later, race-based employment discrimination was banned in the Race Relations Act 1968, which has been amended several times since then. This was followed by an Equal Pay Act in 1970, a Sex Discrimination Act in 1975, and a Disability Discrimination Act in 1995.

MANDLA v LEE

[1983] 2 A.C. 548 (H.L.)

LORD FRASER:

My Lords, the main question in this appeal is whether Sikhs are a "racial group" for the purposes of the Race Relations Act 1976 ("the Act of 1976 "). For reasons that will appear, the answer to this question depends on whether they are a group defined by reference to "ethnic origins."

* * *

Racial group is defined in section 3 (1) of the Act which provides:

> " 'racial group' means a group of persons defined by reference to colour, race, nationality or ethnic or national origins, and references to a person's racial group refer to any racial group into which he falls."

It is not suggested that Sikhs are a group defined by reference to colour, race, nationality or national origins. In none of these respects are they distinguishable from many other groups, especially those living, like most Sikhs, in the Punjab. The argument turns entirely upon whether they are a group defined by "ethnic origins." It is therefore necessary to ascertain the sense in which the word "ethnic" is used in the Act of 1976.* * * The respondent, who appeared on his own behalf, submitted that that was the relevant meaning of "ethnic" in the Act of 1976, and that it did not apply to Sikhs because they were essentially a religious group, and they shared their racial characteristics with other religious groups, including Hindus and Muslims, living in the Punjab.

My Lords, I recognise that "ethnic" conveys a flavour of race but it cannot, in my opinion, have been used in the Act of 1976 in a strictly racial or biological sense. For one thing, it would be absurd to suppose that Parliament can have intended that membership of a particular racial group should depend upon scientific proof that a person possessed the relevant distinctive biological characteristics (assuming that such characteristics exist). The practical difficulties of such proof would be prohibitive, and it is clear that Parliament must have used the word in some more popular sense. For another thing, the briefest glance at the evidence in this case is enough to show that, within the human race, there are very few, if any, distinctions which are scientifically recognised as racial.

* * *

For a group to constitute an ethnic group in the sense of the Act of 1976, it must, in my opinion, regard itself, and be regarded by others, as a distinct community by virtue of certain characteristics. Some of these characteristics are essential; others are not essential but one or more of them will commonly be found and will help to distinguish the group from the surrounding community. The conditions which appear to me to be essential are these: (1) a long shared history, of which the group is conscious as distinguishing it from other groups, and the memory of which it keeps alive; (2) a cultural tradition of its own, including family and social customs and manners, often but not necessarily associated with religious observance. In addition to those two essential characteristics the following characteristics are, in my opinion, relevant; (3) either a common geographical origin, or descent from a small number of common ancestors; (4) a common language, not necessarily peculiar to the group; (5) a common literature peculiar to the group; (6) a common religion different from that of neighbouring groups or from the general community surrounding it; (7) being a minority or being an oppressed or a dominant group within a larger community, for example a conquered people (say, the inhabitants of England shortly after the Norman conquest) and their conquerors might both be ethnic groups.

A group defined by reference to enough of these characteristics would be capable of including converts, for example, persons who marry into the group, and of excluding apostates. Provided a person who joins the group feels himself or herself to be a member of it, and is accepted by other members, then he is, for the purposes of the Act, a member. That appears to be consistent with the words at the end of section 3 (1): "references to a person's racial group refer to any racial group into which he falls." In my opinion, it is possible for a person to fall into a particular racial group either by birth or by adherence, and it makes no difference, so far as the Act of 1976 is concerned, by which route he finds his way into the group. This view does not involve creating any inconsistency between direct discrimination under paragraph (a) and indirect discrimination under paragraph (b). A person may treat another relatively unfavourably "on racial grounds" because he regards that other as being of a particular race, or belonging to a particular racial group, even if his belief is, from a scientific point of view, completely erroneous.

* * *

The result is, in my opinion, that Sikhs are a group defined by a reference to ethnic origins for the purpose of the Act of 1976, although they are not biologically distinguishable from the other peoples living in the Punjab.

LORD TEMPLEMAN:

In the course of the argument attention was directed to the dictionary definitions of the adjective "ethnic." But it is common ground that some definitions constitute the Sikhs a relevant group of ethnic origin whereas other definitions would exclude them. The true construction of the expression "ethnic origins" must be deduced from the Act. A racial group means a group of persons defined by reference to colour, race, nationality or ethnic or national origins. I agree with the Court of Appeal that in this context ethnic origins have a good deal in common with the concept of race just as national origins have a good deal in common with the concept of nationality. But the statutory definition of a racial group envisages that a group defined by reference to ethnic origin may be different from a group defined by reference to race, just as a group defined by reference to national origins may be different from a group defined by reference to nationality. In my opinion, for the purposes of the Race Relations Act a group of persons defined by reference to ethnic origins must possess some of the characteristics of a race, namely group descent, a group of geographical origin and a group history. The evidence shows that the Sikhs satisfy these tests. They are more than a religious sect, they are almost a race and almost a nation. As a race, the Sikhs share a common colour, and a common physique based on common ancestors from that part of the Punjab which is centered on Amritsar. They fail to qualify as a separate race because * * * prior to the inception of Sikhism they cannot be distinguished from other inhabitants of the Punjab. As a nation the Sikhs defeated the Moghuls, and established a kingdom in the Punjab which they lost as a result of the first and second Sikh wars; they fail to qualify as a separate nation or as a separate nationality because their kingdom never achieved a sufficient degree of recognition or permanence. The Sikhs qualify as a group defined by ethnic origins because they constitute a separate and distinct community derived from the racial characteristics I have mentioned. They also justify the conditions enumerated by my noble and learned friend, Lord Fraser of Tullybelton. The Sikh community has accepted converts who do not comply with those conditions. Some persons who have the same ethnic origins as the Sikh have ceased to be members of the Sikh community. But the Sikhs remain a group of persons forming a community recognisable by ethnic origins within the meaning of the Act.

U.K. EQUALITY ACT 2006—OFFICIAL EXPLANATORY NOTES

(available at http://www.opsi.gov.uk/acts/en2006/2006en03.htm)

The Employment Equality (Sexual Orientation) Regulations 2003 (S.I. 2003/1661) and Employment Equality (Religion or Belief) Regulations 2003 (S.I. 2003/1660) made unlawful discrimination on the grounds of sexual orientation and religion or belief in employment and vocational training. These Regulations implement the UK's obligations under the EC Employment Directive (Directive 2000/78/EC). Legislation is also being prepared to prohibit age discrimination in these areas, as required by the Employment Directive. There is currently no statutory institution with responsibility for promoting equality or combating unlawful discrimination in these new equality strands.

Notes and Questions

1. **Meaning of Race Discrimination?** Which of the law lords in Mandla v. Lee best captures the meaning of "race"? Which decision is closer to the U.S. approach? Why is it so difficult to agree on a definition of race?

2. **Influence of EU Law**. Note the influence of EU developments on the law of Great Britain. Is there a similar relation between U.S. fair employment law and state law? Why did Britain not legislate against religious discrimination in employment until 2003? Sexual orientation discrimination until 2003? And why would it take another three years before Britain banned age discrimination in employment?

3. **Definitions.** In the Employment Equality Regulations 2003 (S.I. 2003/1660, 1661) (U.K.), a definition of some of the operative terms is provided:

a. "Sexual orientation" is defined as "a sexual orientation towards—

(a) persons of the same sex;

(b) persons of the opposite sex; or

(c) persons of the same sex and of the opposite sex

b. "Religion or belief" is defined as "any religion, religious belief, or similar philosophical belief."

Do these regulations sufficiently define the protected classes? Would atheists be protected by the religion regulations?

THE EMPLOYMENT EQUALITY (AGE) REGULATIONS 2006

S. I. 2006/1031 (U.K.)

DISCRIMINATION ON GROUNDS OF AGE

3.—(1) For the purposes of these Regulations, a person ("A") discriminates against another person ("B") if—

(a) on grounds of B's age, A treats B less favourably than he treats or would treat other persons, or

(b) A applies to B a provision, criterion or practice which he applies or would apply equally to persons not of the same age group as B, but—

(i) which puts or would put persons of the same age group as B at a particular disadvantage when compared with other persons, and

(ii) which puts B at that disadvantage,

and A cannot show the treatment or, as the case may be, provision, criterion or practice to be a proportionate means of achieving a legitimate aim.

(2) A comparison of B's case with that of another person under paragraph (1) must be such that the relevant circumstances in the one case are the same, or not materially different, in the other.

(3) In this regulation—

(a) "age group" means a group of persons defined by reference to age, whether by reference to a particular age or a range of ages; and

(b) the reference in paragraph (1)(a) to B's age includes B's apparent age.

DISCRIMINATION BY WAY OF VICTIMISATION

4.—(1) For the purposes of these Regulations, a person ("A") discriminates against another person ("B") if he treats B less favourably than he treats or would treat other persons in the same circumstances, and does so by reason that B has—

(a) brought proceedings against A or any other person under or by virtue of these Regulations;

(b) given evidence or information in connection with proceedings brought by any person against A or any other person under or by virtue of these Regulations;

(c) otherwise done anything under or by reference to these Regulations in relation to A or any other person; or

(d) alleged that A or any other person has committed an act which (whether or not the allegation so states) would amount to a contravention of these Regulations,

or by reason that A knows that B intends to do any of those things, or suspects that B has done or intends to do any of them.

(2) Paragraph (1) does not apply to treatment of B by reason of any allegation made by him, or evidence or information given by him, if the allegation, evidence or information was false and not made (or, as the case may be, given) in good faith. * * *

HARASSMENT ON GROUNDS OF AGE

6.—(1) For the purposes of these Regulations, a person ("A") subjects another person ("B") to harassment where, on grounds of age, A engages in unwanted conduct which has the purpose or effect of—

(a) violating B's dignity; or

(b) creating an intimidating, hostile, degrading, humiliating or offensive environment for B.

(2) Conduct shall be regarded as having the effect specified in paragraph (1)(a) or (b) only if, having regard to all the circum-

stances, including in particular the perception of B, it should reasonably be considered as having that effect.

APPLICANTS AND EMPLOYEES

7.—(1) It is unlawful for an employer, in relation to employment by him at an establishment in Great Britain, to discriminate against a person—

(a) in the arrangements he makes for the purpose of determining to whom he should offer employment;

(b) in the terms on which he offers that person employment; or

(c) by refusing to offer, or deliberately not offering, him employment.

(2) It is unlawful for an employer, in relation to a person whom he employs at an establishment in Great Britain, to discriminate against that person—

(a) in the terms of employment which he affords him;

(b) in the opportunities which he affords him for promotion, a transfer, training, or receiving any other benefit;

(c) by refusing to afford him, or deliberately not affording him, any such opportunity; or

(d) by dismissing him, or subjecting him to any other detriment.

(3) It is unlawful for an employer, in relation to employment by him at an establishment in Great Britain, to subject to harassment a person whom he employs or who has applied to him for employment.

(4) Subject to paragraph (5), paragraph (1)(a) and (c) does not apply in relation to a person—

(a) whose age is greater than the employer's normal retirement age or, if the employer does not have a normal retirement age, the age of 65; or

(b) who would, within a period of six months from the date of his application to the employer, reach the employer's normal retirement age or, if the employer does not have a normal retirement age, the age of 65.

(5) Paragraph (4) only applies to a person to whom, if he was recruited by the employer, regulation 30 (exception for retirement) could apply.

(6) Paragraph (2) does not apply to benefits of any description if the employer is concerned with the provision (for payment or not)

of benefits of that description to the public, or to a section of the public which includes the employee in question, unless—

(a) that provision differs in a material respect from the provision of the benefits by the employer to his employees; or

(b) the provision of the benefits to the employee in question is regulated by his contract of employment; or

(c) the benefits relate to training.

(7) In paragraph (2)(d) reference to the dismissal of a person from employment includes reference—

(a) to the termination of that person's employment by the expiration of any period (including a period expiring by reference to an event or circumstance), not being a termination immediately after which the employment is renewed on the same terms; and

(b) to the termination of that person's employment by any act of his (including the giving of notice) in circumstances such that he is entitled to terminate it without notice by reason of the conduct of the employer.

(8) In paragraph (4) "normal retirement age" is an age of 65 or more which meets the requirements of section 98ZH of the 1996 Act.

EXCEPTION FOR GENUINE OCCUPATIONAL REQUIREMENT ETC.

8.—(1) In relation to discrimination falling within regulation 3 (discrimination on grounds of age)—

(a) regulation 7(1)(a) or (c) does not apply to any employment;

(b) regulation 7(2)(b) or (c) does not apply to promotion or transfer to, or training for, any employment; and

(c) regulation 7(2)(d) does not apply to dismissal from any employment, where paragraph (2) applies.

(2) This paragraph applies where, having regard to the nature of the employment or the context in which it is carried out—

(a) possessing a characteristic related to age is a genuine and determining occupational requirement;

(b) it is proportionate to apply that requirement in the particular case; and

(c) either—

(i) the person to whom that requirement is applied does not meet it, or

(ii) the employer is not satisfied, and in all the circumstances it is reasonable for him not to be satisfied, that that person meets it.

CONTRACT WORKERS

9.—(1) It is unlawful for a principal, in relation to contract work at an establishment in Great Britain, to discriminate against a contract worker—

(a) in the terms on which he allows him to do that work;

(b) by not allowing him to do it or continue to do it;

(c) in the way he affords him access to any benefits or by refusing or deliberately not affording him access to them; or

(d) by subjecting him to any other detriment.

(2) It is unlawful for a principal, in relation to contract work at an establishment in Great Britain, to subject a contract worker to harassment.

(3) A principal does not contravene paragraph (1)(b) by doing any act in relation to a contract worker where, if the work were to be done by a person taken into the principal's employment, that act would be lawful by virtue of regulation 8 (exception for genuine occupational requirement etc.).

(4) Paragraph (1) does not apply to benefits of any description if the principal is concerned with the provision (for payment or not) of benefits of that description to the public, or to a section of the public to which the contract worker in question belongs, unless that provision differs in a material respect from the provision of the benefits by the principal to his contract workers.

(5) In this regulation—

"principal" means a person ("A") who makes work available for doing by individuals who are employed by another person who supplies them under a contract made with A;

"contract work" means work so made available; and

"contract worker" means any individual who is supplied to the principal under such a contract.

Notes and Questions

1. **"Victimisation"**. Is the U.K.'s prohibition of victimisation broader than the prohibition of retaliation in section 704 of the Civil Rights Act of 1964, 42 U.S.C. § 2000e–3 or in the ADEA, 29 U.S.C. § 623(d)?

2. **Treatment of Age Bias**. How, if at all, is the prohibition of age discrimination different than under the ADEA? Is age-based man-

datory retirement now barred in the U.K.? Is there a greater latitude for employers to engage in age bias with respect to the hiring of retirement-eligible workers? Is the "genuine occupational requirement" exception materially different from the "bona fide occupational qualification" concept under the ADEA, 29 U.S.C. § 623(f)(1)?

3. **Treatment of Contract Workers**. Note also the provisions dealing with "contract workers". How, if at all, is this issue handled under U.S. law?

C. OTHER EUROPEAN COUNTRIES

Europe has a long tradition of regulating the employment relationship. And the notion of equality appears in national constitutions, dating back to the French Declaration of the Rights of Man and of the Citizen in 1789:

> Article 1, Men are born and remain free and equal in respect of rights.
>
> Article 2, France.... shall ensure the equality of all citizens before the law, without distinction of origin, race or religion.

This idea was expanded to include women, after World War II. "The Preamble to the French Constitution of 1946 ... states in general terms that 'the law shall guarantee women equal rights with men in all spheres." Folke Schmidt, Discrimination Because of Sex, in Discrimination in Employment: A study of Six Countries by the Comparative Labour Law Group 142 (Folke Schmidt, ed. 1978) [hereafter "Study of Six Countries"]. A 1972 law required employers to provide men and women equal pay for equal work or work of equal value. Under the influence of the 2000 EU employment directives, France has enacted "a general regime prohibiting discrimination on the basis of race and origin, whether direct and indirect, in all areas covered by Directive 2000/43, general provisions prohibiting discrimination are transversal and cover not only the grounds covered by Article 13 of the Amsterdam Treaty but also physical appearance, last name, customs, health, political opinions, trade union activities and involvement in mutual benefit organizations, family situation and genetic characteristics." Sophie Lawrence, Executive summary 2005: French country report on measures to combat discrimination, p. 2 (Migration Policy Group, 2006) (available at www.migpolgroup.com/infopages/3481.html).

In the German Works Councils Act of 1920, guidelines agreed upon by the council and the employer must provide 'that the hiring of an employee may not depend upon his political opinion, his belief, or his trade union activity, or on his membership or non–membership of a political, religious or professional association or a military organization. They may not require that employment shall depend upon belonging to a certain sex' (Art. 81, § 1). A similar rule concerned dismissals (Art. 84, § 1 subsec. 1).“ Thilo Ramm, Introduction, in A Study of Six Countries, supra, at 4. Germany responded to the 1976 EU gender equality directive by enacting Civil Law Code § 611a, “which prohibits employers from discriminating on the basis of sex.” Raphael Won–Pil Suh & Richard Bales, German and European Employment Discrimination Policy, 9 Oregon Rev. Intl. L. 261 (2006). Responding to the 2000 EU employment directives, Germany enacted a comprehensive anti-discrimination law, the General Equal Treatment Act of 2006, (Allgemeines Gleichbehandlungsgesetz, BGBl I 2006, 1897), which reaches discrimination on account of race or ethnic origin, sex, religion or philosophy of life, disability, age, or sexual identity, as well as a separate prohibition of harassment.

D. ASIA

1. Japan

Japan's two principal areas of difficulty concern discrimination against female workers and age-based mandatory retirement. In both areas, there is legislation on the books but significant questions still persist over whether employers comply with anti-discrimination strictures.

HIROYA NAKAKUBO, “PHASE III” OF THE JAPANESE EQUAL EMPLOYMENT OPPORTUNITY ACT

4 Japan Labor Rev. 9 (No. 3, Summer 2007)

Presently in Japan, more than 40% of all employed persons (more precisely, 22.8 million or 41.6% of 54.7 million employees) are women, with female workers comprising more than 40% of the entire labor force population. * * *

From a social perspective, it is imperative that female workers not be excluded simply because of their gender. They should be provided with equal opportunities to exercise their capability to perform important roles at work. For the purpose of establishing gender-equal workplaces, the Japanese Equal Employment Opportunity Act (hereinafter referred to as the “EEOA”) was enacted in 1985 and took effect in April of the following year.

Prior to this act, although Article 14 of the Constitution clearly stipulated the prohibition of discrimination on the basis of sex, it was construed as not directly applicable to private employment relations. The only provision relating this principle to employment issues was Article 4 of the Labor Standards Act (hereinafter referred to as the “LSA”), which prohibits wage discrimination between male and female workers. Sex discrimination regarding loss of employment was outside the reach of Article 4, but Japanese courts, invoking Article 90 of the Civil Code which nullifies a contractual provision repugnant to "the public order and good morals of the society," struck down some types of unfavorable measures against women, such as the "retirement on marriage" rule and the lower mandatory retirement age.

It was certainly a commendable effort on the part of judiciary to realize the spirit of the Constitution in the workplace. However, as for the stage of recruitment and hiring, the Supreme Court, in contrast to its attitude towards employment termination, emphasized that a wide range of freedom should be given to employers, allowing them even to make discriminatory selections unless there is a specific statutory ban.

Thus, a policy of employing only men for main career positions on the career advancement track was widespread, and women were often hired for ancillary positions with inferior educational background. Even when there was a wage differential between male and female workers, the employer could easily argue that they did not engage in equivalent work, thereby severely limiting the functions of Article 4 of the LSA.

The purpose of adopting the EEOA was to rectify such situations, as well as to ratify the United Nations Convention on the Elimination of All Forms of Discrimination against Women (1979). However, the legislative movement met with strong opposition that it conflicted with the traditional employment practices and the social values of Japan. As a result, the original EEOA became a product of compromise, wherein, for example, employers were only obligated to "endeavor" to treat men and women equally during the recruiting and hiring processes. The law was therefore criticized for being lukewarm and ineffective, but substantial strides were made with the 1997 revisions (implemented in April 1999). They reinforced provisions for equality, such as a square mandate of equal treatment at the time of recruitment and hiring, and added special provisions pertaining to sexual harassment.

Then, in June 2006, more than 20 years after the enactment of the EEOA, a bill requiring further major revisions was passed by the Diet, and took effect on April 1 of this year. The current revisions achieved significant development with a move from prohibiting discrimination against women to prohibiting "discrimination on the basis of sex." At the same time, new provisions were added to prohibit so-called indirect discrimination and to protect female workers from pregnancy-related discrimination. * * *

In the current revisions, the most important issue affecting the nature of the law is a change from "discrimination against women" to "discrimination on the basis of sex," which applies to both men and women. * * *

[Eds. Professsor Nakakubo highlights Articles 5, 7, 9 and 11 of the 2006 Act, for which he provides translations:]

Article 5. (Prohibition of Discrimination on the Basis of Sex)

With regard to the recruitment and hiring of workers, employers shall provide equal opportunities for all persons regardless of sex.

Article 6

With regard to the following matters, employers shall not discriminate against workers on the basis of sex.

(i) Assignment (including allocation of duties and grant of authority), promotion, demotion, and training of workers;

(ii) Loans for housing and other similar fringe benefits as provided by Ordinance of the Ministry of Health, Labor and Welfare;

(iii) Change in job type and employment status of workers; and

(iv) Encouragement of retirement, mandatory retirement age, dismissal, and renewal of the labor contract.

Article 7. (Measures on the basis of Conditions other than Sex)

An employer shall not take measures concerning the recruitment and hiring of workers or any of the matters listed in the items of the preceding Article which apply a criterion concerning a person's condition other than the person's sex and which are specified by the Ordinance of the Ministry of Health, Labor and Welfare as measures that may cause a discrimination in effect by reason of sex, considering the proportion of men and women who satisfy the criterion and other matters, except in cases where there is a legitimate reason to take such measures, such as where said measures are specifically required for the purpose of performing the relevant job in light of the nature of that job, or cases where such measures are specifically required for the purpose of employment management in light of the circumstances of the conduct of the employer's business.

* * *

Article 9. (Prohibition, etc. of Disadvantageous Treatment by Reason of Marriage, Pregnancy, Childbirth, etc.)

(1) Employers shall not stipulate marriage, pregnancy or childbirth as a reason for retirement of women workers.

(2) Employers shall not dismiss women workers for marriage.

(3) Employers shall not dismiss or give disadvantageous treatment to women workers by reason of pregnancy, childbirth, or for requesting absence from work as prescribed in Article 65, para-

graph 1, of the Labor Standards Act (Act No. 49 of 1947), or having taken absence from work as prescribed in the same Article, paragraph 1 or 2, of the same act, or by other reasons relating to pregnancy, childbirth as provided by Ordinance of the Ministry of Health, Labor and Welfare.

(4) Dismissal of women workers who are pregnant or in the first year after childbirth shall be void. However, this shall not apply in the event that the employer proves that the dismissal in question was not for reasons prescribed in the preceding paragraph.

Article 11. (Employment Management Measures Concerning Problems Caused by Sexual Speech or Behavior in the Workplace)

(1) Employers shall establish necessary systems in terms of employment management to counsel workers and cope with their problems, and take other necessary measures so that workers they employ do not suffer any disadvantage in their working conditions by reason of said workers' responses to sexual speech or behavior in the workplace and that their working environments do not suffer any harm due to such sexual speech or behavior.

JAPAN LAW CONCERNING STABILIZATION OF EMPLOYMENT OF OLDER PERSONS

Law No. 68 of May 25, 1971, as amended

Article 8. In cases where the employer fixes the retirement age of his or her employees, * * * the retirement age shall not be below 60. Provided, this shall not apply to workers employers by said employers that are in occupations recognized by [the] Ministry of Health, Labour and Welfare * * * as occupations difficult for older persons to fulfill.

Article 9. In cases where the employer fixes the retirement age (limited to under 65 years old * * *), he or she shall conduct any one of the measures listed in the items below in order to secure stable employment for older workers until the age of 65 * * *:

(1) Raising the retirement age;

(2) Introduction of a continuous employment system (refers to the system of continuing to employ an older person wishing to be employed following said employee's retirement * * *);

(3) Abolition of the retirement age. * * *

Notes and Questions

1. **Effect on Mandatory Retirement?** Evaluate the incentives that the legislature attempted to provide in Article 9 of the older workers law. Is age-based retirement likely to wither away?

2. **Is Race and Ethnicity Discrimination Unregulated?** Note that despite the gradual expansion of coverage and tightening of the non-discrimination laws, discrimination in hiring based on race or ethnicity is not forbidden in Japan, even though Japan is a party to the International Convention on the Elimination of All Forms of Racial Discrimination. Doudou Diène, the rapporteur for a United Nations commission, has observed:

> that there is racial discrimination and xenophobia in Japan, and that it affects three circles of discriminated groups: the national minorities—the Buraku people, the Ainu and the people of Okinawa; people and descendants of former Japanese colonies—Koreans and Chinese; foreigners and migrants from other Asian countries and from the rest of the world. The manifestations of such discrimination are first of all of a social and economic nature. All surveys show that minorities live in a situation of marginalization in their access to education, employment, health, housing, etc. Secondly, the discrimination is of a political nature: the national minorities are invisible in State institutions. Finally, there is profound discrimination of a cultural and historical nature, which affects principally the national minorities and the descendants of former Japanese colonies. This is mainly reflected in the poor recognition and transmission of the history of those communities and in the perpetuation of the existing discriminatory image of those groups.
>
> Concerning the policies and measures adopted by public authorities, the Special Rapporteur welcomes the adoption of a number of laws which promote certain rights of certain minorities, but notes with concern that the there is no national legislation that outlaws racial discrimination and provides a judicial remedy for the victims.

U.N. Commission on Human Rights, Racism, Racial Discrimination, Xenophobia and All Forms of Discrimination (2006) (available at www.debito.org/UNdienereport012406.html).

What might account for the disparity between Japan's treatment of sex and age discrimination and the treatment of race and ethnicity discrimination? Note that Japan has adopted a law protecting the disabled, which includes, in Section 16, this language:

> 1. The Government and the local governments shall take positive measures to promote employment of persons with disabilities in respect of specific jobs and areas that are suitable for persons with disabilities.

2. Employers shall make efforts to secure employment of persons with disabilities through evaluating their abilities properly, providing appropriate workplaces and proper employment management on the basis of social solidarity.

3. The Government and the local governments shall take necessary measures for employers of persons with disabilities to promote and maintain their employment through subsidizing employers' costs for adjustments of the facilities and equipment necessary for employment of persons with disabilities.

§ 16 of the Basic Law for Persons with Disabilities, Law No. 84 of 21 May 1970 (last amended in June 2004). How does this approach to disability discrimination compare with the approach used in other countries?

2. China

1994 CHINA LABOR LAW

(trans. from China Daily, 6 July 1994, p. 2)

Section 3. Labourers shall have the right to be employed on an equal basis, choose occupations, obtain remuneration for their labour, take rest, have holidays and leaves, obtain protection of occupational safety and health, receive training in vocational skills, enjoy social insurance and welfare, and submit applications for settlement of labour disputes, and other rights relating to labour as stipulated by law.

* * *

Section 12. Labourers shall not be discriminated against in employment, regardless of their ethnic community, race, sex, or religious belief.

Section 13. Females shall enjoy equal rights as males in employment. It shall not be allowed, in the recruitment of staff and workers, to use sex as a pretext for excluding females from employment or to raise recruitment standards for the females, except for the types of work or posts that are not suitable for females as stipulated by the State.

Section 14. Where there are special stipulations in laws, rules and regulations on the employment of the disabled, the personnel of national minorities, and demobilized army men, such special stipulations shall apply.

Section 15. No employing units shall be allowed to recruit juveniles under the age of 16.

* * *

Section 29. The employing unit shall not revoke its labour contract with a labourer in accordance with the stipulations in section 26 and section 27 of this Law in any of the following circumstances:

(1) to be confirmed to have totally or partially lost the ability to work due to occupational diseases or injuries suffered at work;

(2) to be receiving medical treatment for diseases or injuries within the prescribed period of time;

(3) to be a female staff member or worker during pregnant, puerperal, or breast-feeding period; or

(4) other circumstances stipulated by laws, administrative rules and regulations.

* * *

Section 58. The State shall provide female workers and juvenile workers with special protection. "Juvenile workers" hereby refer to labourers at the age of 16 but not 18 yet.

Section 59. It is prohibited to arrange female workers to engage in work down the pit of mines, or work with Grade IV physical labour intensity as stipulated by the State, or other work that female workers should avoid.

Section 60. Female workers during their menstrual period shall not be arranged to engage in work high above the ground, under low temperature, or in cold water or work with Grade III physical labour intensity as stipulated by the State.

Section 61. Female workers during their pregnancy shall not be arranged to engage in work with Grade III physical labour intensity as stipulated by the State or other work that they should avoid in pregnancy. Female workers pregnant for seven months or more shall not be arranged to extend their working hours or to work night shifts.

Section 62. After childbirth, female workers shall be entitled to no less than 90 days of maternity leaves with pay.

Section 63. Female workers during the period of breast-feeding their babies less than one year old shall not be arranged to engage in work with Grade III physical labour intensity as stipulated by the State or other labour that they should avoid during their breast-feeding period, or to extend their working hours or to work night shifts.

VOICES AGAINST DISCRIMINATION: CHINESE CITIZENS CHALLENGE DISCRIMINATORY PRACTICE

China Law and Governance Review (Issue No. June 2004)
(available at www.chinareview.info/issue2)

China's labor market, in which demand for jobs far outstrips supply, means that employers get to call the shots. In November 2003, nearly 10,000 people applied for 600 civil service positions offered by the Beijing municipal government (Beijing Evening News, November 13, 2003) while 36,000 applicants vied for 7,900 civil service positions in the central government and other state-level government offices (Beijing Morning Post, November 3, 2003). For rural migrants from poorer regions, almost any job is acceptable. To make things worse, workers and job applicants have few places to turn to for redress against discriminatory practices. Although Article 12 of China's Labor Law .expressly prohibits discrimination based on race, nationality, sex and religious belief, no other laws or regulations exist for enforcing such anti-discrimination provision. Nor is there any mechanism for victims of employment discrimination not specifically prohibited by law to seek any legal remedy. * * *

One need to look no further than the information required in a typical job application form to understand the extent of the problem: name, sex, age, ethnicity, education, place of birth, family background, height, health, work experience, plus a picture of the applicant—each could be used and has been used by Chinese employers as grounds for discrimination. An anecdote widely circulated in the Chinese press describes an able young job applicant who was refused a job because her last name was Pei (aè), which in Chinese has the same pronunciation as the word for losing money. Below is a closer look at some of the areas where widespread employment discrimination exists today.

Gender

Despite the express prohibition against gender discrimination under the PRC Labor Law, discrimination against women is among the most flagrant in China's job market. The government itself continues to maintain different retirement ages for male and female civil servants. The long-standing government policy of "equal pay for equal work" for men and women, which had propelled a high percentage of Chinese women into the workforce, has not stopped women from being forced out of failing state-owned enterprises at a higher rate than men. * * * For the younger generation, the entry barrier for female college graduates seemed to have received the most media attention. During each hiring season, reports such as the following Xinhuanet story begin to surface: a job fair in Beijing for female college graduates was cancelled when only five companies accepted the invitations sent out to 500 companies nationwide. According to the event's sponsors, many of the companies contacted openly declared their unwillingness to hire female graduates. * * * At the Capital Normal University in Beijing, 70% of the 2003 graduates who had not found jobs by August that year were women. Those fortunate enough to land jobs reported more difficult job searches than men and many had to settle for less desirable positions. As a result, more women now choose to remain in school to pursue higher degrees. (Xinhuanet, August 26, 2003) Many employers justify their discriminatory practices on the ground that the child-bearing age of young women increases labor costs and that "females in general are less creative and aggressive than men". (Xinhuanet, December 24, 2002) Some employers even require young female graduates to agree not to have children within a number of years after their hiring. (Chinanews.com, July 15, 2003).

Residency

China's household registration system, under which all citizens are assigned either a rural or urban resident classification based on their parents' origin, has effectively relegated the millions of rural men and women who have migrated to cities seeking work to second class status. While they are eagerly recruited—and exploited—for work in the construction and hygiene industries and other low-paying manual labor jobs, they are banned from most other occupations. For example, in 1996, the Beijing Labor Bureau issued a directive under which only 12 out of 204 listed occupations in Beijing were open to migrant workers. * * *

In addition, state benefits which are taken for granted by urban workers—education through high school, medical care, unemployment insurance—are not available to migrant workers or their families during their stay in cities. As Zhang Shuguang, Executive Director of the Unirule Institute of Economics, a leading independent think-tank in Beijing, pointed out, the household registration system has "created two different pay scales in the labor market of urban and economically developed areas. On the one hand is the labor market for locals, which, in addition to wages, provides housing, social security, education and training. On the other hand is the labor market for migrant workers, which does not provide any benefits other than wages. Despite the repeated increases in wages and benefits for urban workers, the migrant workers' wages and benefit status remain unchanged. ("From Free

Movement of Labor to Freedom of Movement for the Population" 29%, March 10, 2002, www.unirule.org.cn).

AGE

In today's job market, age discrimination is no longer reserved for China's old. Thousands of middle-aged workers who have been laid off from failing state-owned enterprises now must seek reemployment. Many employers, however, are only willing to consider much younger job applicants. According to one study, 82% of the employers surveyed imposed an age requirement of 35 and below. Only 1% of them did not impose any age requirement. (Source: The Top Tens of 2003, the Beijing Publishing House, 2004). * * *

HEIGHT, WEIGHT AND PHYSICAL APPEARANCE

* * * Most of the same local governments that reject [Hepatitis B] carriers from their civil service positions also impose height and weight requirements. In Anhui Province, males must be no less than 160 cm (5 ft. 3 in.) in height and weigh no less than 50 kilograms (110 pounds) and females must be no less than 152 cm (5 ft.) in height and weigh no less than 40 kilograms (88 pounds). Hunan Province requires its male civil servants to be at least 160 cm (5 ft. 3 in.) in height and weigh no less than 45 kilograms (99 pounds) and females to be above 150 cm (4 ft. 11 in.) in height and weigh no less than 40 kilograms (88 pounds). (Sources: China Financial Times, April 8, 2003 and February 13, 2004).

Notes and Questions

1. For a good general review, see Ronald Brown, China's Employment Discrimination Laws During Economic Transition, 19 Colum. J. Asian L. 361 (2006).

2. Can employment discrimination laws be effective without strong enforcement mechanisms? What accounts for the lack of strong enforcement mechanisms in China?

E. SOUTH AFRICA

EMPLOYMENT EQUITY ACT 1998

CHAPTER II. PROHIBITION OF UNFAIR DISCRIMINATION

6. Prohibition of unfair discrimination

(1) No person may unfairly discriminate, directly or indirectly, against an employee, in any employment policy or practice, on one or more grounds, including race, gender, sex, pregnancy, marital status, family responsibility, ethnic or social origin, colour, sexual

orientation, age, disability, religion, HIV status, conscience, belief, political opinion, culture, language and birth.

(2) It is not unfair discrimination to—

(a) take affirmative action measures consistent with the purpose of this Act; or

(b) distinguish, exclude or prefer any person on the basis of an inherent requirement of a job.

(3) Harassment of an employee is a form of unfair discrimination and is prohibited on any one, or a combination of grounds of unfair discrimination listed in subsection (1).

Notes and Questions

1. Note that the definition of employee includes applicants for employment.

2. Is the concept of "unfair discrimination" a useful one?

3. What reasons support banning employment discrimination based on conscience, belief, political opinion, culture? Are these types of discrimination tolerated in many other countries, including the United States? If so, why?

F. MEXICO

ANNA TORRIENTE, MINIMUM EMPLOYMENT STANDARDS IN MEXICO

(National Law Center for Inter–American Free Trade, Sept. 1995)
(available at www.natlaw.com./pubs/torrient.htm)

SOURCES OF LAW

A. Constitutional Law

Article 123, Title 6 of the Mexican Constitution establishes minimum employment standards in Mexico, including working hours, minimum wages and compensation for improper dismissals. Section A governs relations between employers and employees in general, whereas Section B establishes the rights of employees of the federal government and of the Federal District.

B. The Federal Labor Law

The Federal Labor Law (Ley Federal de Trabajo) is the regulatory law implementing the constitutional protections established in Constitutional Article 123. The Federal Labor Law (hereinafter "FLL") was originally enacted on August 18, 1931 and has been amended on various occasions * * *. The Federal Labor Law is applicable in all of the states of the Republic of Mexico. Neither the individual states nor the Federal District have enacted state legislation governing the area of labor.

* * *

Composition of the Work Force

Article 7 requires Mexican employers to employ at least 90% Mexican workers in their enterprises. All technical and professional workers must be Mexican, unless there are no Mexican workers qualified in a particular specialty. In that case, the employer may employ foreign workers, but only to the extent of 10% of the labor force engaged in the specialty. It is then incumbent upon the employer and the foreign workers to train the Mexican workers in the specialty. All doctors in the service of employers must be Mexican nationals.

Article 7 is not applicable to directors (CEOs), administrators and general managers. (Note: NAFTA Chapter 16 permits exchanges of workers between the NAFTA countries as long as there is reciprocity.)

* * *

The Work Contract: Pursuant to FLL Article 25, the written contract of work conditions must specify:

1—The name, age, nationality, sex, marital status and address of the worker and employer;

2—Whether the employment relation is for a specific task or for a specific period or without limit of time;

3—The service or services to be rendered (to be indicated with specificity);

4—The place or places where the work is to be performed;

5—The working hours;

6—The nature and amount of wages;

7—The date and place of payment of wages;

8—A declaration that the worker will be trained in accordance with the established procedures of the enterprise and in accordance with the terms of the labor laws; and

9—Other working conditions, such as rest days, vacations and other issues upon which the worker and employer may agree.

Employment Abroad: Extra protection is provided to a Mexican national who contracts to work for a foreign employer for foreign work or work on foreign soil. First, the labor contract must be signed by a competent municipal authority and countersigned by the consul of the nation to which the employer is to go. In addition to the ordinary specifications to be contained in the contract, it must clearly specify that the expense of repatriating the employee should be borne by the foreign employer.

Where employers use intermediaries to contract workers, the employer remains responsible for all obligations. Such workers have the same rights as regularly employed workers and the intermediaries may not take a commission or charge fees from their salaries.

Agreements Prohibited by Operation of Law: The Constitution expressly prohibits the inclusion of certain terms and conditions in a labor contract. Where included in a contract, the following conditions will be considered null and void and of no binding effect upon the parties:

* * * The Employment of Women: FLL Article 164 provides that women shall have the same rights and obligations as men. Constitutional Article 123 (A)(VII) establishes the principle of equal pay for equal work regardless of gender. Nevertheless, the labor laws establish a special protective scheme for maternity. FLL Article 166 provides that, when the health of a woman or her fetus/child would be endangered during the pregnancy or nursing period, she may not engage in unhealthy or dangerous labor, night industrial work or work in commercial or service establishments after 10 o'clock at night. These rights are without prejudice to the female employee's salary, benefits and other rights under her employment agreement. This prohibition, however, has the effect of denying the female employee the ability to earn greater income by forbidding her from working overtime.

Pregnant Employees: Women during pregnancy may not perform physical labor requiring considerable effort and which could be hazardous to their health.

Maternity Leave: Pregnant employees are entitled to six weeks' leave prior to the approximate date of childbirth and to six weeks' leave thereafter. During this time period, they are entitled to receive their full wages and retain their employment and the rights acquired under their labor contract. During the nursing period, nursing mothers are entitled to two extra paid half-hour rest periods for nursing their children. (Constitutional Article 123(A)(V); FLL Article 170, paras. II, IV and V). The six weeks' maternity leave may be extended to the time necessary if it is impossible for the female worker to return to work due to her pregnancy or postnatal recovery. During the regular six week maternity leave, the female worker is entitled to her full wages. In the case of extended maternity leave, the worker will be entitled to half pay for no more than 60 days. (FLL Article 170). With regard to paid maternity leave, the Mexican Social Security Institute (

Instituto Mexicano de Seguridad Social, hereinafter "IMSS") subsidizes 60% of the female worker's salary; therefore, the employer need only pay the difference.

The IMSS provides nursery services for children of workers from 43 days to 4 years of age. (FLL Article 171). This system was established as a social service charged against the IMSS and was published in the Diario Oficial on March 23, 1973. Finally, FLL Article 172 requires the employer to provide a sufficient number of chairs for working mothers. In fact, this is an obligation the employer owes to the workers regardless of sex or maternal/gestational status. (FLL Article 132 (V)).

* * *

Equal Pay: Equal wages must be paid for equal work, regardless of sex or nationality. (Constitutional Article 123 (A)(VII)).

Notes and Questions

1. Is Mexico's protective legislation consistent with the objective of sex equality in the workplace?

2. Is the Mexican ban on pay discrimination based on nationality more expansive than U.S. law?

Chapter Three

DEFINITION OF UNLAWFUL DISCRIMINATION

Once the legislature decides to forbid discrimination based on a classification such as race, sex, disability, etc., the next issue is how to define unlawful discrimination. Bans on discrimination commonly forbid actions taken with a discriminatory purpose. Here, the issue becomes how to prove purpose. A ban on discrimination may also encompass actions that have a discriminatory effect. Does "comparable worth" fit under either category? Finally, may employers turn to affirmative action to increase employment of previously excluded groups?

A. FACIAL DISCRIMINATION

An employer may seek to justify seemingly forbidden classifications on the ground that are real differences between members of different groups. For example, the employer may believe that members of one sex are more likely to be the family "breadwinners" than another. Or the employer may point to differences in legal status, life expectancy, reproductive organs, linguistic background, or perceived ability to do the job. To what extent do such actual or perceived differences justify facially discriminatory actions?

SKYRAIL OCEANIC LTD. v COLEMAN

[1981] ICR 864 (C.A.)

Lawton L.J.

This is an appeal by Mrs. Rosalind Coleman, who is a young married woman now aged 21, against that part of a judgment of the Employment Appeal Tribunal that set aside a finding of an industrial tribunal that she had been unlawfully discriminated against under the Sex Discrimination Act 1975.

The facts out of which the appeal arises are unusual. On August 1, 1977, the appellant, who was then a spinster aged 17, began work as a booking clerk with the respondents, who trade as Goodmos Tours. They are travel agents, specialising in chartering aircraft for tourist flights to Israel. They have been engaged in this kind of business for some years. The appellant in the course of her work was bound to get to know of business information that would be of value to rival firms, some of whom engaged in trade espionage. In March 1978, when she was 18, she became engaged to the man whom she married on September 5, 1978. He worked for a rival firm of travel agents, Travel the World Ltd., who wanted to undertake charter flights to Israel. She announced her engagement. News of it disturbed the respondents' managing director, a Mr. Mozes. He appreciated the possibility that she might divulge information about the respondents' business to her finance. He had a talk with her, stressing the need for confidentiality, and said that if she did divulge information he would sack her. She promised not to do so. She continued in her employment.

There were two leakages of information from the respondents in July 1978. One was to Travel the World Ltd. The appellant was not accused at the time of being the source of the leaks, nor was any suggestion to that effect made before the industrial tribunal. There was some evidence that, when her engagement became known, some senior members of the respondents' staff told Mr. Mozes that he ought to dismiss her because of the danger of leaks. About that time, Mr. Mozes's son had a talk with a director of Travel the World Ltd., a Mr. Levinson. Neither were called as witnesses, but Mr. Mozes said this about the talk:

> "... [Mr. Levinson] told my son of the engagement of the applicant and her present husband. He said it would not be fair to carry on as we were as we would be accusing one another of leakages."

Mr. Mozes attended the wedding on September 5, 1978. The next day, he dismissed the appellant by letter, giving her two weeks' pay in lieu of notice. The explanation that he gave for dismissing her was as follows:

> "Regretfully I have to come to the conclusion that it would not be fair to your husband in his position to keep you employed in a similar capacity competing in the same business and dealing with the same clientele. Neither would it be fair to yourself nor to the respective companies."

He added a postscript: "For your information Mr. Levinson of Travel the World has spoken to us about the same problem and is of the same opinion."

On December 4, 1978, the appellant made an application to an industrial tribunal alleging unfair dismissal. * * *

The industrial tribunal heard the application on October 3 and 4, 1979, and decided that the respondents had discriminated against the appellant unlawfully within the meaning of the Act of 1975 and that she had been unfairly dismissed. They awarded her £1,666 compensation, of which £1,000 was for injury to feelings. They found that she had been dismissed because she was a woman instead of being a man, which was discrimination within section 1 (1) (a) of the Act of 1975. That finding was based on what the respondents had put in their answer and what Mr. Mozes had said when giving evidence.

The Employment Appeal Tribunal adjudged that there had been no discrimination under section 1 (1) (a) of the Act of 1975. They decided as they did on the ground that there had been no material on which the industrial tribunal could have concluded that the respondents had treated the appellant less favourably than they treated, or would have treated, a man employed by them in the same situation.

* * *

I am satisfied that the dismissal of a woman based on an assumption that men are more likely than women to be the primary supporters of their spouses and children can amount to discrimination under the Act of 1975.

The problem that [attorney for appellant] Mr. Lester had to overcome in this case was that the respondents had had a reason for dismissing the appellant that had had nothing to do with her sex. What mattered to them was the fact that she was on intimate terms with an employee of a rival firm. Mr. Lester submitted, however, that what had triggered off their decision to dismiss the appellant was their assumption that her husband would be the breadwinner after their marriage. It was that that had led them to treat her less favourably than they would have treated a man in their employment who happened to have a wife working for a rival firm.

* * *

[Attorney for respondent] Mr. Burke–Gaffney said that, in order to find out whether the respondents would have treated the appellant less favourably than a man, the court had to envisage a situation in which a rival firm employed a wife whom they were reluctant to dismiss. In that situation, on the evidence the respondents would have dismissed the husband, and such dismissal would have had nothing to do with sex. What is wrong with that argument, as Mr. Lester pointed out in his reply, is that there is no evidence that the rival firm were reluctant to dismiss Mr. Coleman. All that the industrial tribunal decided was that Mr. Coleman was employed by the rival firm. There was evidence that the respondents and Mr. Levinson of the rival firm had discussed the problem arising from the fact that they were employing a married couple. Following that discussion, the appellant had been dismissed because of the assumption that was made. * * *

Mr. Burke–Gaffney also submitted that the evidence did not establish that the respondents had discriminated against the appellant on the ground of her sex. The assumption that they had made had had no sexual connotation because a breadwinner could be of either sex. That is so, but, in the circumstances of this case, the assumption was that husbands were breadwinners and wives were not. Such an assumption is, in my judgment, based on sex. On the issue of liability, I would allow the appeal.

ROBERTS v TATE & LYLE INDUSTRIES LTD.

[1986] ICR 371 (E.C.J.)

2. The questions were raised in the course of proceedings between the applicant, Joan Roberts, and Tate & Lyle Industries Ltd., previously Tate & Lyle Food and Distribution Ltd. (hereinafter referred to as "Tate & Lyle"), concerning the question whether the applicant's dismissal was in accordance with section 6(4) of the Sex Discrimination Act 1975 and with Community law.

3. The applicant was employed by Tate & Lyle at their Liverpool depot for 28 years and, at the age of 53, was made redundant on 22 April 1981, following the closure of the depot, together with other employees, under a mass redundancy.

4. The applicant was a member of an occupational pension scheme, which had been created in 1978 by Tate & Lyle for their employees and which was contracted out of the state retirement pension scheme. That scheme is funded partly by Tate & Lyle themselves and partly by voluntary contributions by employees. It provides for compulsory retirement with a pension at the age of 65 for men and 60 for women. Nevertheless, men and women over the age of 50 may, with Tate & Lyle's consent, retire before attaining the aforementioned normal retirement age, in which case they are entitled to a reduced pension immediately. An employee who has been a member of the scheme for 10 years may choose to retire at

any time up to five years before the normal retirement age and receive the pension earned up to that date.

5. On the closure of the Liverpool depot Tate & Lyle agreed [on] severance terms with the trade union of which the applicant was a member. Under those terms all employees made redundant were to be offered either a cash payment or an early pension out of the pension scheme up to five years before the date of their entitlement under the scheme. The pension was therefore payable immediately to women over the age of 55 and men over the age of 60. Nevertheless, as a result of representations made by male employees against the allegedly discriminatory nature of those arrangements with regard to men aged between 55 and 60, Tate & Lyle amended them by agreeing to grant an immediate pension to both men and women over the age of 55, with the amount of their cash payment reduced.

6. The applicant, who was aged 53 at the date of redundancy, brought proceedings against Tate & Lyle before an industrial tribunal, claiming that her dismissal constituted unlawful discrimination contrary to the Sex Discrimination Act 1975 and to Community law, since under the new arrangements, a male employee was entitled to receive an immediate pension 10 years before the normal retirement age for men whereas a female employee was not so entitled until five years before the normal retirement age for women.

* * *

18. By the first question the Court of Appeal seeks to ascertain whether article 5(1) of Directive No. 76/207 must be interpreted as meaning that a contractual provision which lays down a single age for the dismissal of both men and women under a mass redundancy involving the grant of an early retirement pension, whereas the normal retirement age is different for men and women, namely 65 for the former and 60 for the latter, constitutes discrimination on grounds of sex contrary to that directive.

19. The applicant considers that the first question must be answered in the affirmative.

20. According to her the question falls to be considered, by virtue of the court's judgment of 16 February 1982, Burton v. British Railways Board (Case 19/81) [1982] I.C.R. 329, under Directive No. 76/207. The terms "working conditions" and "conditions governing dismissal" contained in that directive also encompass the grant of an early retirement pension under a mass redundancy.

* * *

22. The applicant claims that she is entitled, according to the judgment in the *Burton* case, to compare her treatment with that of a male employee who is an equal number of years away from the normal retirement age. A scheme which applies an age differential with regard to the retirement of men and of women, and which departs from that differential in the case of a mass redundancy in a manner less favourable to women than to men, gives rise to discrimination on grounds of sex, contrary to the provisions of directive.

* * *

25. According to Tate & Lyle, a woman cannot demand to be treated differently in all cases for the sole reason that there is a difference in treatment with regard to the normal retirement age applied by the employer under its occupational social security scheme. On the contrary, such a difference of treatment should not be reflected in other matters prior to the normal date of retirement.

26. The fact that the court held in its judgment in the *Burton* case that a difference in the age which men and women must have attained for access to voluntary retirement cannot be regarded as discrimination does not mean, according to Tate & Lyle, that identical age conditions are necessarily discriminatory. In any event, the treatment applied in this case is justified objectively by the need to ensure that all employees who are dismissed and are over the age of 55 receive a pension.

* * *

30. The court observes in the first place that the question of interpretation which has been referred to it does not concern the conditions for the grant of the normal old-age or retirement pension but the termination of employment in connection with a mass redundancy caused by the closure of part of an undertaking's plant. The question therefore concerns the conditions governing dismissal and falls to be considered under Directive No. 76/207.

31. Article 5(1) of Directive No. 76/207 provides that application of the principle of equal treatment with regard to working conditions, including the conditions governing dismissal, means that men and women are to be guaranteed the same conditions without discrimination on grounds of sex.

32. In its judgment in the *Burton* case the court has already stated that the term "dismissal" contained in that provision must be given a wide meaning. Consequently, an age limit for the compulsory redundancy of workers as part of a mass redundancy falls within the term "dismissal" construed in that manner, even if the redundancy involves the grant of an early retirement pension.

33. Even though the retirement scheme at issue does not prima facie discriminate between men and women with regard to the conditions for dismissal, it is still necessary to consider whether the fixing of the same age for the grant of an early pension nevertheless constitutes discrimination on grounds of sex in view of the fact that under the United Kingdom statutory social security scheme the pensionable age for men and women is different. Under United Kingdom legislation the minimum qualifying age for a state retirement pension is 60 for women and 65 for men.

34. As the court emphasised in its judgment in the *Burton* case, article 7 of Council Directive (79/7/E.E.C.) expressly provides that the directive does not prejudice the right of member states to exclude from its scope the determination of pensionable age for the purposes of granting old-age and retirement pensions and the possible consequences thereof for other benefits falling within the statutory social security schemes. The court thus acknowledged that benefits linked to a national scheme which lays down a different minimum pensionable age for men and women may lie outside the ambit of the aforementioned obligation.

35. However, in view of the fundamental importance of the principle of equality of treatment, which the court has reaffirmed on numerous occasions, article 1(2) of Directive No. 76/207, which excludes social security matters from the scope of that directive, must be interpreted strictly.

Consequently, the exception to the prohibition of discrimination on grounds of sex provided for in article 7(1)(a) of Council Directive (79/7/E.E.C.) applies only to the determination of pensionable age for the purposes of granting old-age and retirement pensions and to the consequences thereof for other social security benefits.

36. In that respect it must be emphasised that, whereas the exception contained in article 7 of Council Directive (79/7/E.E.C.) concerns the consequences which pensionable age has for social security benefits, this case is concerned with dismissal within the meaning of article 5 of Directive No. 76/207. In those circumstances the grant of a pension to persons of the same age who are made redundant amounts merely to a collective measure adopted irrespective of the sex of those persons in order to guarantee them all the same rights.

37. Consequently, the answer to the first question referred to the Court of Justice by the Court of Appeal must be that article 5(1) of Directive No. 76/207 must be interpreted as meaning that a contractual provision which lays down a single age for the dismissal of men and women under a mass redundancy involving the grant of an early retirement pension, whereas the normal retirement age is

different for men and women, does not constitute discrimination on grounds of sex, contrary to Community law.

COMMISSION OF THE EUROPEAN COMMUNITIES v FRENCH REPUBLIC

[1988] E.C.R. 3559 (Case 318/86)

2. The dispute concerns the system of recruitment to the civil service in France. It is common ground that under French legislation, the only criterion for recruitment is a candidate' s grading after a single-entry competition open to both men and women. However, Article 21 of Law No 84–16 of 11 January 1984 laying down statutory rules on the State public service * * * provides that for certain corps of officials, a list of which is to be drawn up by decree, separate recruitment may be organized for men and women. Those recruitment procedures are characterized by the fact that each decision ordering the holding of a competition fixes the percentage of posts to be allotted to men and women respectively.

* * *

9. With regard to management, technical and vocational training staff in the external departments of the prison service, the French Government admits that the derogation provided for in the national legislation is not in conformity with the directive. It has announced its intention to remove that corps from the contested list.

10. The issue between the parties is therefore limited to the requirements of the directive in relation to head warders of prisons and to the five corps in the national police force.

(a) Head warders responsible for the direction of prisons

* * *

12. As far as custodial staff in general are concerned, the Commission admits that the specific nature of the post of warder and the conditions under which warders carry out their activities justify reserving such posts primarily for men in male prisons and primarily for women in female prisons. To that extent, the different access to the custodial staff corps arising from a system of separate recruitment for men and women does not go beyond the limits laid down in Article 2 (2) of the directive.

13. However, the Commission considers that an exception should be made in the case of 'surveillants chefs' in charge of prisons. They carry out management functions which involve no regular contact with the prisoners. Their duties are thus comparable to those of a 'directeur d' etablissement' (governor of a penal

institution), the only difference residing in the capacity of the penal institution managed by the official concerned. * * *

16. The question to be considered accordingly concerns a corps in respect of which separate recruitment of male and female candidates is regarded as justified under Article 2 (2) of the directive, in which promotion is carried out without discrimination but in which promotion to the highest grade may, in certain cases, lead to a situation in which the person concerned carries out activities of such a nature that sex does not constitute a determining factor.

17. In such a situation, the derogation provided for in Article 2 (2) of the directive extends to activities corresponding to the highest grade of the corps concerned, even if certain of those activites do not necessarily have to be carried out by persons of one sex. Although it is true, as the Commission has emphasized, that the French authorities could have avoided the problem by organizing their departments differently, for example by creating a separate corps for prison governors, or by including that post in the management staff corps, it must also be admitted that there could be reasons for appointing to the post of head warder only persons having actually performed the duties of a warder. However, the French Government gave the Court to understand that such reasons exist in this case, having regard to the need to provide for opportunities for promotion within the corps of warders and to the fact that the professional experience acquired in that corps is desirable for the performance of the duties of a prison governor. For its part, the Commission has not shown that those arguments are not valid.

18. The Commission' s complaints relating to head warders responsible for the direction of prisons must therefore be rejected.

(b) THE FIVE CORPS IN THE NATIONAL POLICE FORCE

23. The argument conducted before the Court showed that the two parties agree that certain activities connected with the duties performed by the corps of the national police force may be performed by men only or, depending on the case, by women only, whereas certain other duties may be performed by any member of the police force, whether male or female. The dispute concerns the consequences arising from such a situation in relation to the application to Article 2 (2) of the directive.

24. In that regard, it should be pointed out that Article 2 (2) of the directive leaves the Member States the power to exclude certain 'occupational activities' from its field of application and that Article 9 (2) of the directive requires them periodically to assess the

activities in question in order to decide, in the light of social developments, whether there is justification for maintaining the exclusions concerned. Article 9 (2) further provides that the Member States are to notify the Commission of the results of that assessment.

25. It follows from those provisions that the exceptions provided for in Article 2 (2) may relate only to specific activities, that they must be sufficiently transparent so as to permit effective supervision by the Commission and that in principle they must be capable of being adapted to social developments. The last requirement gives rise to no difficulties in this case; however, French law is not in accordance with the other two requirements.

26. As regards the requirement of transparency, it must be concluded that it is not fulfilled. Under the system of separate recruitment, the percentages of posts to be allotted to men and women respectively are fixed in the decision ordering the holding of a competition; the fixing of those percentages is not governed by any objective criterion defined in a legislative provision.

27. This lack of transparency also has consequences for compliance with the second requirement laid down by the directive, which relates to the activities involved. The contested system of recruitment makes it impossible to exercise any form of supervision, not only by the Commission and the courts but also by persons adversely affected by discriminatory measures, in order to verify whether the percentages fixed for the the recruitment of each sex actually correspond to specific activities for which the sex of the persons to be employed constitutes a determining factor within the meaning of Article 2 (2) of the directive.

* * *

29. Consequently, the Commission' s complaints concerning the system of recruiting officials to the five corps of the national police force must be upheld.

30. It follows from the foregoing that by retaining in force a system of separate recruitment according to sex, contrary to the requirements of Council Directive 76/207/EEC, for appointment to the management staff corps and the corps of technical staff and vocational training staff in the external departments of the prison service as well as to all of the five corps in the national police corps, the French Republic has failed to fulfil its obligations under the Treaty. The remainder of the application must be dismissed.

TOTTENHAM GREEN UNDER FIVE'S CENTRE v MARSHALL (NO. 2)

[1991] ICR 320 (E.A.T.)

Knox J.

* * * The issue between the parties * * * issue revolved around the provisions of section 5 and in particular 5(1)(a) and 5(2)(d) [of the Racc Relations Act of 1976], which provide:

> "(1) In relation to racial discrimination—
>
> (a) section 4(1)(a) or
>
> (c) does not apply to any employment where being of a particular racial group is a genuine occupational qualification for the job; . . .
>
> (2) Being of a particular racial group is a genuine occupational qualification for a job only where— . . .
>
> (d) the holder of the job provides persons of that racial group with personal services promoting their welfare, and those services can most effectively be provided by a person of that racial group."

The industrial tribunal on that first occasion held that "exception," to use the description in the side note to section 5, did not apply and on that footing there was no doubt but that there had been discrimination within section 4(1)(a).

It is necessary to state the setting in which the issue arises. The respondent to the original application and the appellant before us, Tottenham Green Under Five's Centre ("the Centre"), runs a nursery for two to five year olds which has largely Afro–Caribbean children. At the relevant time the percentage was 84 per cent. and there was an advertisement for a worker which led indirectly to the applicant applying for the job. He did not, on his evidence, in fact see the advertisement but he heard about the job and applied for it.

He is white and not Afro–Caribbean. After he had been told that he would be interviewed, he was told when it was learnt that his ethnic background was English and that he was white, that he need not attend for interview. It was on that that he based his claim that he had been discriminated against, contrary to section 4(1)(a).

* * *

The appeal is primarily based on the findings that were made by the industrial tribunal on the second occasion and the conclusion that was drawn in relation to those findings. What was said on this score was as follows:

> "5. . . . We accept that the requirement was for the nursery assistant to provide a number of personal services to the children.
>
> "6. There is a general agreement that these personal services were: (1) maintaining the cultural background link for the children of the Afro–Caribbean background; (2) dealing with the parents and discussing these matters with them; (3) reading and talking where necessary in dialect; (4) generally looking to their skin and health and including the plaiting of their hair."

* * *

Continuing with the industrial tribunal's decision we find this in paragraph 8:

> "we accept that an Afro–Caribbean is more likely to be able to speak a West Indian dialect than someone from a different ethnic origin and would therefore most effectively provide this service."

At that stage we have three features; (1) an acceptance that there were personal services required for the post; (2) that those personal services included reading and talking where necessary in dialect; (3) an acceptance that an Afro–Caribbean would most effectively provide this service. Subsequently, however, the industrial tribunal drew a distinction between that particular service, reading and talking where necessary in dialect, and the other three in the list in paragraph 6 of the decision quoted above. In relation to reading and talking where necessary in dialect they said:

> "in our view this particular requirement was the least emphasised of the four. We believe that an applicant who fulfilled the other requirements listed and who had no ability to speak or read the dialect would not have been precluded from getting the post. We knew, for example, that the applicant had no such ability and yet it had been proposed to call him for interview. Also this requirement is not mentioned in the job advertisement or in the job description. It is in the nature of a desirable extra and no more."

* * *

[T]he industrial tribunal have stated the way in which the ability to read and talk where necessary in dialect was viewed in contra-distinction to the other personal services. There is a perfectly clear finding that the other three could most effectively be provided by any trained nursery assistant, and no question therefore arises of our finding any error of law in that respect. With regard to the ability to read and talk where necessary in dialect, we have as we have explained above, a finding of fact which is binding upon us, that was as it is variously described, a desirable extra; a requirement that could be dispensed with and not a requirement that was rated as fundamental to the post or an integral requirement with the other three.

* * *

What remains is a relatively unimportant and not trivial duty and we have reached the conclusion that it is not the correct view of the meaning of this paragraph that the industrial tribunal can make an evaluation of the importance of the duty in question and disregard it although it is satisfied that it is something that is not so trivial that it can properly be disregarded altogether. It seems to us that subsection (3) indicates clearly that one of the duties of the job if it falls within any of the relevant paragraphs, in our case paragraph (d) of the preceding subsection, will operate to make the exception available. That is what one can discern that Parliament intended to provide.

There is no suggestion at all that one has to look to see whether some duties are more important than others, and once one reaches that conclusion, it seems to us, that as a matter of law it is not an answer to a reliance on section 5(2)(d) that a relevant duty is either only a desirable extra, or something that could be dispensed with, or something which is not fundamental to the post. It is still one of the duties of the job and in those circumstances, it not being trivial and it being genuine, it seems to us that the exception necessarily did apply.

This is one of those exceptional cases where we can, in our view, substitute our view for that of the industrial tribunal because in this very careful decision we do find very clearly set out the relevant factual background and all that is effectively left is the legal conclusion from that factual background. We therefore allow this appeal and substitute a decision that there was no discrimination contrary to section 4(1)(a) of the Race Relations Act 1976.

Notes and Questions

1. **Employer's Options?** Would Skyrail and Travel the World Ltd. have violated the Sex Discrimination Act if they had required Coleman and her husband to disclose who was the principal bread winner and then fired the employee who was not the principal bread winner? Or if they had required the couple to choose which one was to lose his or her job? If they had fired both employees?

2. **Influence of Persisting Sex Differentials in Retirement Age?** Is it possible to secure the non-discrimination principle across-the-board when the state allows sex distinctions in retirement age?

3. **BFOQ?** Should the Commission have conceded that sex distinctions in the hiring of warders are justified? Would sex be a "bona fide occupational qualification" (BFOQ) in an American prison? Is Article 2(2) equivalent to the U.S. BFOQ provision?

4. **Race–Based BFOQ?** Suppose Marshall spoke fluently in a West Indian dialect. Would the genuine occupational qualification exception still apply? If not, is it legitimate to assume that he is less fluent than an Afro–Caribbean? Is it wise to allow a BFOQ exception in race cases? Note that there is no race-based BFOQ in Title VII.

B. ASCERTAINING DISCRIMINATORY PURPOSE (DIRECT DISCRIMINATION)

BARTON v INVESTEC HENDERSON CROSTHWAITE SECURITIES LTD.

[2003] IRLR 332 (E.A.T.)

His Honour Judge Ansell:

1. This is an appeal from a Decision of an Employment Tribunal sitting at London Central who, following a hearing held in June 2002, by a Reserved Decision promulgated on 30 September 2002, unanimously held that:

> (1) the Respondent had proved that the variation in salary and [long-term investment plans (LTIP)] between the Appellant and her comparator, Mr. Matthew Horsman, was genuinely due to a material factor which was not the difference of sex.
>
> (2) Difference in treatment between the Appellant and Matthew Horsman in relation to the grant of share options was due to a material factor which was not the difference of sex for the purposes of the Equal Pay Act or, if the share options were not regulated by the contract of employment, did not amount to less favourable treatment of the Applicant on the grounds of her sex.
>
> (3) The Respondents did not treat the Appellant less favourably on the grounds of sex in awarding bonuses.

* * *

3. The Appellant, aged fifty two at the time of the hearing, has twenty three years' experience in the fund management and broking investment banking fields, and in particular, twenty years as a respected media expert. She joined the Respondents as an analyst in June 1990, and by the late 1990s she had become their

Research Director. She was particularly successful in the old style of backroom analysis, but said to be less happy with the more modern role of the analyst involving a high profile image for both herself and her employer. Over the years, she had also involved herself in stock sales for her clients, although, again, the modern trend was towards concentrating sales with specialist salesmen. The Tribunal found that the Appellant's way of doing her own sales was not appreciated or encouraged by senior management. The Tribunal's conclusion was, however, that the Appellant had a genuinely high profile in a limited specialist media context, but less so in the developing broader media world of broadcasting and the internet.

4. The Respondents employ a hundred and fifty staff, comprising forty in credit finance, forty in sales, forty in research and the rest in support functions. They are a subsidiary of a larger organisation, Investec Bank UK, who are themselves linked to Guinness Mahon and the Bank of Yokohama. Their only witness before the Tribunal was Perry Crosthwaite, the Chairman, and the person who the Tribunal found was very much the key figure in the setting of salaries and other benefits and bonuses. The Tribunal found that the four elements to the final package of the employees concerned in these events comprised the basic salary, a bonus awarded at the end of the financial year, share options and LTIPs. LTIPs are amounts awarded but paid over a period of time between two to four years, whose principal aim is to keep valuable employees within the organisation.

5. Matthew Horsman joined the Respondents on 1 January 1997 as a Research Director, having previously been a respected financial journalist with The Independent newspaper. The Appellant had been actively involved in his recruitment. In the years after his arrival, the Appellant and Mr. Horsman pooled their bonuses, although they were not necessarily shared. By June or July 1999 the Tribunal found that Mr. Crosthwaite had been made aware that there were attempts being made by other organisations to poach Mr. Horsman. He was desperate not to lose him as he was regarded as one of the three key members of staff within the organisation. At that time, both he and the Appellant were on a basic salary of £105,000, and a decision was made to increase Mr. Horsman's salary to £150,000 and to award him an LTIP of £75,000. Further, in December 1999, he was granted 12,000 share options, whereas the Appellant only received 7,500. It is these three aspects of pay that give rise to the claim under the Equal Pay Act, although, as we have already indicated, the Tribunal were unsure as to whether or not share options fell within the ambit of the Equal Pay Act.

6. By early 2001, the Appellant had been given information in relation to the possible disparity of salaries between her and Mr. Horsman; that information did not extend to the disparity as regards share options or LTIPs. As a result of a complaint to her employers, they increased her salary from April 2001 to £150,000, the same as Mr. Horsman, but said nothing to her about the other aspects of salary. She only found out about those matters much later in the year, once proceedings had been commenced. The other main issue in the case relates to the setting of bonuses. The Tribunal held that after 1998 bonuses were less closely based on the revenue produced by the particular employee. The determination as to what factors were taken into account with regard to bonus setting after that date, and the nature of the process involved are very much at the heart of this case.

7. Michael Savage joined the media term as a specialist media salesperson in June 2000, having fourteen years' experience in the City and trained both as a Research Analyst and then developed specialist sales skills. The Tribunal found that the Respondents saw him as a very valuable acquisition, combining sales, analytical organisational and client-handling skills, and to secure him they offered him a salary of £150,000 and an LTIP of £150,000 per annum for two years, and a guaranteed minimum bonus of £50,000, although the LTIP element in the remuneration did involve some compensation for benefits that he had lost from his previous employment. He was not the comparator for equal pay purposes, since the Tribunal held, and it is not disputed, that he was not involved in like work with the Appellant. The Tribunal also held, although the issue had been a matter of some argument within the Tribunal hearing, that Mr. Savage was put in charge of the team at the end of 2000. They found that the Appellant had received this news badly and became increasingly non-cooperative, declining to contribute to a team budget and compiling her own.

8. The Sex Discrimination Act claim arises from the award of the 2001 budget in the spring of that year. The Tribunal found that in the Respondents' bonus setting was:

> "a rough and ready process, not a precise science. It was not a paper based exercise."
>
> They also spoke of an:
>
> "underlying philosophy of avoiding precision and written material to prevent giving individuals the material on which they could challenge their bonuses."

The bonuses awarded in the spring of 2001 were £1 million to Mr. Horsman, £600,000 to Mr. Savage and £300,000 to the Appellant. It is said that she had generated revenue of £3.2 million, Mr. Savage £5.3 million and Mr. Horsman £10 million. There was considerable cross-examination in the Tribunal as to respects in which the Appellant's figures had been undervalued and Mr. Savage's overvalued. The Appellant's complaint was in relation to the differential between her bonus and that of Michael Savage, particularly as he had been in the organisation for only ten months of the bonus year.

* * *

PROOF OF DISCRIMINATION—BURDEN OF PROOF

* * *

25. We . . . consider it necessary to set out fresh guidance in the light of the statutory changes:

> (1) Pursuant to section 63A of the Sex Discrimination Act 1975 [(SDA)], it is for the Applicant who complains of sex discrimination to prove on the balance of probabilities facts from which the Tribunal could conclude, in the absence of an adequate explanation, that the Respondents have committed an act of discrimination against the Applicant which is unlawful by virtue of Part 2 or which by virtue of section 41 or 42 SDA is to be treated as having been committed against the Applicant. These are referred to below as "such facts"
>
> (2) If the Applicant does not prove such facts he or she will fail.
>
> (3) It is important to bear in mind in deciding whether the Applicant has proved such facts that it is unusual to find direct evidence of sex discrimination. Few employers would be prepared to admit such discrimination, even to themselves. In some cases the discrimination will not be an intention but merely based on the assumption that "he or she would not have fitted in".
>
> (4) In deciding whether the Applicant has proved such facts, it is important to remember that the outcome at this stage of the analysis by the Tribunal will therefore usually depend on what inferences it is proper to draw from the primary facts found by the Tribunal.
>
> (5) It is important to note the word is "could". At this stage the Tribunal does not have to reach a definitive determination that such facts would lead it to the conclusion that there was an act of unlawful discrimination. At this stage a Tribunal is looking at the primary facts proved by the Applicant to see what inferences of secondary fact could be drawn from them.
>
> (6) These inferences can include, in appropriate cases, any inferences that it is just and equitable to draw in accordance

with section 74(2)(b) of the Sex Discrimination Act from an evasive or equivocal reply to a questionnaire or any other questions that fall within section 74(2) of the Sex Discrimination Act see Hinks v. Riva Systems EAT/501/96.

(7) Likewise, the Tribunal must decide whether any provision of any relevant code of practice is relevant and if so, take it into account in determining such facts pursuant to section 56A(10) SDA. This means that inferences may also be drawn from any failure to comply with any relevant code of practice.

(8) Where the applicant has proved facts from which inferences could be drawn that the Respondents have treated the Applicant less favourably on the grounds of sex, then the burden of proof moves to the respondent.

(9) It is then for the respondent to prove that he did not commit, or as the case may be, is not to be treated as having committed that act.

(10) To discharge that burden it is necessary for the respondent to prove, on the balance of probabilities, that the treatment was in no sense whatsoever on the grounds of sex, since "no discrimination whatsoever" is compatible with the Burden of Proof Directive.

(11) That requires a Tribunal to assess not merely whether the respondent has proved an explanation for the facts from which such inferences can be drawn, but further that it is adequate to discharge the burden of proof on the balance of probabilities that sex was not any part of the reasons for the treatment in question.

(12) Since the facts necessary to prove an explanation would normally be in the possession of the respondent, a Tribunal would normally expect cogent evidence to discharge that burden of proof. In particular the Tribunal will need to examine carefully explanations for failure to deal with the questionnaire procedure and/or code of practice.

26. We now deal with two matters of law raised in relation to the Equal Pay Act. The Tribunal set out in paragraph 60 of their Decision the test to be satisfied to establish the material factor defence as set out in Brunnhofer v. Bank der osterreichischen Postsparkasse AC [2001] ECR 4961 and Bilka–Kaufhaus GmbH v. Webers Von Hartz [1987] ICR 110. Mr. Allen submits, therefore, that the burden was on the Respondents to prove:

(1) that there were objective reasons for the difference;

(2) unrelated to sex;

(3) corresponding to a real need on the part of the undertaking;

(4) appropriate to achieving the objective pursued;

(5) it was necessary to that end;

(6) that the difference conformed to the principle of proportionality;

(7) that was the case throughout the period during which the differential existed.

We agree with [appellant's] submissions on this point as to the seven factors correctly identified by the Tribunal.

29. Having attempted to determine the difficult issues of law that arise in this case, how do our decisions impact on the Tribunal's findings?

30. Dealing with transparency, the Appellant's substantial complaint was in relation to certain paragraphs of the Decision . . . wherein the Tribunal found and appeared to condone, in part relying on their "industrial knowledge", that the City "bonus culture" was one of secrecy and lack of transparency. The Tribunal's alleged "industrial knowledge" of this culture certainly conflicted with the lay members of this Court, who had experience of many large institutions operating transparent bonus systems, including formal end of year appraisals, followed by a properly documented bonus setting procedure. This Court would certainly wish to make it clear that no Tribunal should be seen to condone a City bonus culture involving secrecy and/or lack of transparency because of the potentially large amounts involved, as a reason for avoiding equal pay obligations. Mr. Allen highlighted the Tribunal's findings in relation to "the backdrop of an unwritten, non transparent bonus policy in an organisation, without an appraisal system, without an equal opportunities policy" coupled with the Tribunal's findings that they were not satisfied that the Respondents had given all discovery possible on the topic. The Respondents had not produced any documents relating to the process of determination of the bonuses; there was no documentation as to the determination of the salary increase and LTIP increases for Mr. Horsman, or the basis upon which the amount of those increases had been determined. The Tribunal had observed, concerning Mr. Crosthwaite's evidence:

> "He was not forthcoming either in the conduct of the litigation or in the course of evidence as to pay differentials and reasons for them"

* * *

32. We are, therefore, quite satisfied that there was an abundance of primary fact material from which the Tribunal could, and indeed should, have drawn inferences, in the absence of an adequate explanation from the Respondents, such that they could conclude that an act of discrimination had been committed and that therefore the burden of proof was placed upon the Respondents to prove that sex was not a reason for the less favourable treatment in relation to the bonus setting.

33. [S]ince the Tribunal clearly did not, in our view, deal with the matter in the required two-stage process as we have indicated, we would propose to remit the matter to a fresh Tribunal for them to reconsider the matter.

34. * * * Bearing in mind the background to this case to which we have already made reference, namely the lack of transparency and the serious failure to deal with the questionnaire process, these were important factors which the Tribunal failed to take into account when assessing the material factor defence. In particular, the Tribunal failed properly to deal with (1) whether the Respondents had proved that there were objective reasons for the difference (2) the issues of proportionality, and (3) whether there was a real need on the part of the business for those differences existing throughout the period of the difference, i.e. between 1999 and 2001, particularly in the light of the Respondents' willingness in April 2001, following a complaint from the Appellant, to increase her salary level to that of Mr. Horsman without his salary then being further increased. Accordingly in relation to the equal pay claim we propose to allow the appeal and direct a re-hearing before a different Tribunal.

DRISKEL v PENINSULA BUSINESS SERVICES LTD.

[2000] IRLR 151 (E.A.T.)

Mr. Justice Holland:

1. Mrs. Driskel is now aged 56. In May 1994 she commenced employment with Peninsula Business Services Ltd ("Peninsula") as an Advice Line Consultant. Peninsula provide advice and advocacy services in connection with employment; seemingly Mrs. Driskel gave advice by telephone. In September 1995 Mr. Huss became head of her department. As head Mr. Huss was unpopular for various reasons with all or many of the persons in the department and with the passage of time there was a growing antipathy to him on the part of Mrs. Driskel, which antipathy became mutual. Says Mrs. Driskel, Mr. Huss had a penchant for sexual banter and comments and she specifies incidents that involved them both as arising in respectively February 1996 (twice), April 1996 and June

1996. On the 4th June 1996 there was advertised the post of Senior Advice Line Consultant (effectively the deputy to Mr. Huss). Only Mrs. Driskel applied—Mr. Huss's preferred candidate did not apply. On the 11th July there was a further incident involving Mr. Huss and Mrs. Driskel; on the 12th July the former interviewed the latter for the post. The process was not brought to a proper conclusion: Mrs. Driskel left the interview room and initiated a complaint of sexual harassment. Mr. Done, as a managing director of Peninsula, deputed Mr Sutcliffe, Director of Consultancy, to investigate and deal with the complaint. There was some delay in reporting which led to Mrs. Driskel initiating a formal grievance on the 28th August—in the event the day on which Mr. Sutcliffe reported so as to reject her complaint. There followed much 'toing and froing' with the upshot that Mrs. Driskel refused to work even as Senior Advice Line Consultant unless Mr. Huss moved elsewhere. He refused to move; Peninsula took the view that he could not be made to do so. Given impasse, Peninsula dismissed Mrs. Driskel for "some other substantial reason" on the 20th October 1996 with one month's pay in lieu of notice. [She brought suit under the Sex Discrimination Act, and the lower court [Industrial Tribunal] ruled against her.] The Employment Appeal Tribunal reversed. The Industrial Tribunal should have followed Reed and Bull Information Systems Ltd. v. Stedman (1999) 1 RCR 299 at 302:

> It is particularly important in cases of alleged sexual harassment that the fact finding tribunal should not carve up the case into a series of specific incidents and try (to) measure the harm or detriment in relation to each.

* * *

10. * * * [T]he Tribunal's approach should be as follows:

a. The Tribunal hears the evidence and finds the facts. As has already been pointed out it is desirable not to include in this exercise judgments as to the discriminatory significance, if any, of individual incidents—judgment thus far should be limited to the finding of all facts that are prima facie relevant. If ad hoc assessments 'discrimination or no' are made the result is a fragmented and discursive judgment; more importantly, there is the potential noted in *Reed and Bull* for ignoring the impact of totality of successive incidents, individually trivial.

b. The Tribunal then makes a judgment as to whether the facts as found disclose apparent treatment of the female applicant by the Respondents as employers in one or more of the respects identified in Section 6(2)(a) and (b) [of the Sex

Discrimination Act of 1975] that was less favourable than their treatment, actual or potential, of a male employee.

c. The Tribunal further considers any explanation put forward on behalf of the Respondent employers. In the light of any such explanation is the discrimination so far potentially identified, real or illusory?

d. In making judgments under b. and c. above (and in practice these two stages may elide together) the following guidance is applicable:

(1) Sexual harassment is helpfully categorised in *Reed and Bull*:

> It seems to us important at the outset that 'sexual harassment' is not defined by statute. It is a colloquial expression which describes one form of discrimination in the workplace made unlawful by s.6 of the Sex Discrimination Act 1975. Because it is not a precise or defined phrase, its use, without regard to s.6, can lead to confusion. Under s.6 it is unlawful to subject a person to a 'detriment' on the grounds of their sex. Sexual harassment is a shorthand for describing a type of detriment. The word detriment is not further defined and its scope is to be defined by the fact-finding tribunal on a common-sense basis by reference to the facts of each particular case. The question in each case is whether the alleged victim has been subjected to a detriment and, second, was it on the grounds of sex.

(2) The finding of less favourable treatment leading to "detriment" is one of fact and degree so that a single act may legitimately found a complaint.

* * *

(4) In making its judgment a Tribunal should not lose sight of the significance in this context of the sex of not just the complainant but also that of the alleged discriminator. Sexual badinage of a heterosexual male by another such cannot be completely equated with like badinage by him of a woman. Prima facie the treatment is not equal: in the latter circumstance it is the sex of the alleged discriminator that potentially adds a material element absent as between two heterosexual men.

(5) Throughout the Tribunal should remain conscious of the burden and standard of proof. That said, the notion that discrimination may well be covert and is not readily

admitted is as applicable in the content of sex as in the context of race.

13. Had the Tribunal so directed itself as to the law would it nonetheless have dismissed the complaint made pursuant to the Sexual Discrimination Act 1975? We are confident that the answer is 'no'.

* * *

b. We turn to the crucial incident of the 10th July 1996. In our judgment had the Tribunal correctly directed itself as to the law it would first, have sought to put the incident in context, that is, as the latest in a line of incidents with "its predecessors". Second, it would readily have found that that which was complained of amounted prima facie to discrimination of a high order. She was in the unenviable position of having to seek promotion by way of a one to one interview with a man for whom she had an antipathy. In such circumstances she was in receipt of remarks that in an appalling fashion sought to exploit the situation by reference to the sex of, respectively, interviewee and interviewer. [T]hat which was complained of was objectively prima facie discriminatory and it would need some exceptional findings to negate that inference by reference to the respective perceptions of Mrs. Driskel and Mr. Huss. As it was, the Tribunal was heavily influenced by, Mrs. Driskel's failure to make an immediate complaint without reminding itself that any instinct to complain must perforce be inhibited by the fact that she wanted the promotion that would come from the approval of Mr. Huss—and that she did in fact complain on the day following when she perceived that she had no chance of promotion. Further and in any event, given the nature of the remarks how significant was any failure to complain? Turning to Mr. Huss, the Tribunal's finding that the remark was flippant and was not meant to be taken seriously effectively misses the point. It is irrelevant that he never expected her to turn up for the interview in sexually provocative dress—what is relevant is that by this remark (flippant or not) he was undermining her dignity as a woman when, as a heterosexual, he would never similarly have treated a man. Again, the Tribunal seriously misdirected itself in putting any weight on Mr. Huss's sexual vulgarity towards male employees for the reasons already set out in this judgment, that is, that being heterosexual that which he said was to men was vulgar without being intimidatory.

Notes and Questions

1. **Transparency?** Should lawyers advise employers to adopt transparent pay systems? What would a transparent system entail?

2. **Burden of Persuasion**. Compare the burden of persuasion in an English fair employment case and a U.S. case.

3. **Lower Court's Error in *Driskel*?** What was the lower court's error in *Driskel*? Did Mr. Huss also engage in sexual harassment of men?

C. DISCRIMINATORY EFFECT

BILKA-KAUFHAUS GmbH v WEBER VON HARTZ

[1987] ICR 110 (E.C.J.)

3. It appears from the documents before the court that for several years Bilka, which belongs to a group of department stores in the Federal Republic of Germany employing several thousand persons, has had a supplementary (occupational) pension scheme for its employees. This scheme, which has been modified on several occasions, is regarded as an integral part of the contracts of employment between Bilka and its employees.

4. According to the version in force since 26 October 1973, part-time employees may obtain pensions under the scheme only if they have worked full-time for at least 15 years over a total period of 20 years.

5. Mrs. Weber was employed by Bilka as a sales assistant from 1961 to 1976. After initially working full-time, she chose to work part-time from 1 October 1972 until her employment came to an end. Since she had not worked full-time for the minimum period of 15 years, Bilka refused to pay her an occupational pension under its scheme.

* * *

24. In the first of its questions the national court asks whether a staff policy pursued by a department store company excluding part-time employees from an occupational pension scheme constitutes discrimination contrary to article 119 where that exclusion affects a far greater number of women than men.

* * *

26. In that judgment the court considered the question whether the payment of a lower hourly rate for part-time work than for full-time work was compatible with article 119.

27. Such a practice is comparable to that at issue before the national court in this case: Bilka does not pay different hourly rates to part-time and full-time workers, but it grants only full-time workers an occupational pension. Since, as was stated above, such a pension falls within the concept of pay for the purposes of the

second paragraph of article 119 it follows that, hour for hour, the total remuneration paid by Bilka to full-time workers is higher than that paid to part-time workers.

28. The conclusion reached by the court in its judgment of 31 March 1981 is therefore equally valid in the context of this case.

29. If, therefore, it should be found that a much lower proportion of women than of men work full-time, the exclusion of part-time workers from the occupational pensions scheme would be contrary to article 119 of the Treaty where, taking into account the difficulties encountered by women workers in working full-time, that measure could not be explained by factors which exclude any discrimination on grounds of sex.

30. However, if the undertaking is able to show that its pay practice may be explained by objectively justified factors unrelated to any discrimination on grounds of sex there is no breach of article 119.

31. The answer to the first question referred by the national court must therefore be that article 119 of the E.E.C. Treaty is infringed by a department store company which excludes part-time employees from its occupational pension scheme, where that exclusion affects a far greater number of women than men, unless the undertaking shows that the exclusion is based on objectively justified factors unrelated to any discrimination on grounds of sex.

32. In its second question the national court seeks in essence to know whether the reasons put forward by Bilka to explain its pay policy may be regarded as "objectively justified economic grounds," as referred to in the judgment of 31 March 1981, where the interests of undertakings in the department store sector do not require such a policy.

* * *

36. It is for the national court, which has sole jurisdiction to make findings of fact, to determine whether and to what extent the grounds put forward by an employer to explain the adoption of a pay practice which applies independently of a worker's sex but in fact affects more women than men may be regarded as objectively justified economic grounds. If the national court finds that the measures chosen by Bilka correspond to a real need on the part of the undertaking, are appropriate with a view to achieving the objectives pursued and are necessary to that end, the fact that the measures affect a far greater number of women than men is not sufficient to show that they constitute an infringement of article 119.

37. The answer to question 2 (a) must therefore be that under article 119 a department store company may justify the adoption of

a pay policy excluding part-time workers, irrespective of their sex, from its occupational pension scheme on the ground that it seeks to employ as few part-time workers as possible, where it is found that the means chosen for achieving that objective correspond to a real need on the part of the undertaking, are appropriate with a view to achieving the objective in question and are necessary to that end.

Note: EU Directive on Indirect Discrimination

After the decision in *Bilka*, the European Union adopted Directive 97/80, which provides in pertinent part:

DIRECTIVE 97/80

Article 1

Aim

The aim of this Directive shall be to ensure that the measures taken by the Member States to implement the principle of equal treatment are made more effective, in order to enable all persons who consider themselves wronged because the principle of equal treatment has not been applied to them to have their rights asserted by judicial process after possible recourse to other competent bodies.

Article 2

Definitions

1. For the purposes of this Directive, the principle of equal treatment shall mean that there shall be no discrimination whatsoever based on sex, either directly or indirectly.

2. For purposes of the principle of equal treatment referred to in paragraph 1, indirect discrimination shall exist where an apparently neutral provision, criterion or practice disadvantages a substantially higher proportion of the members of one sex unless that provision, criterion or practice is appropriate and necessary and can be justified by objective factors unrelated to sex.

Article 4

Burden of proof

1. Member States shall take such measures as are necessary, in accordance with their national judicial systems, to ensure that, when persons who consider themselves wronged because the principle of equal treatment has not been applied to them establish, before a court or other competent authority, facts from which it may be presumed that there has been direct or indirect discrimina-

tion, it shall be for the respondent to prove that there has been no breach of the principle of equal treatment.

2. This Directive shall not prevent Member States from introducing rules of evidence which are more favourable to plaintiffs.

3. Member States need not apply paragraph 1 to proceedings in which it is for the court or competent body to investigate the facts of the case.

Three years later, in the 2000 directives banning discrimination based on race [2000/43] or religion, disability, age, or sexual orientation [2000/78], the EU slightly modified the definition of indirect discrimination. For example, Article 2 of the race directive provides "indirect discrimination shall be taken to occur where an apparently neutral provision, criterion or practice would put persons of a racial or ethnic origin at a particular disadvantage compared with other persons, unless that provision, criterion or practice is objectively justified by a legitimate aim and the means of achieving that aim are appropriate and necessary." In 2002 Directive 2002/73 adopted similar language regarding sex discrimination.

REGINA v SECRETARY OF STATE FOR EMPLOYMENT, EX PARTE NICOLE SEYMOUR–SMITH AND LAURA PEREZ

[1999] ECR I–00623

[Eds. The plaintiffs challenged a U.K. law that provided that an unfair dismissal case could not be brought until after employees had worked for an employer for two years.]

53. It is common ground that the disputed rule does not entail direct sex discrimination. It must therefore be considered whether the rule may constitute indirect discrimination incompatible with Article 119 of the Treaty.

58. As regards the establishment of indirect discrimination, the first question is whether a measure such as the rule at issue has a more unfavourable impact on women than on men.

59. Next, as the United Kingdom Government was right to point out, the best approach to the comparison of statistics is to consider, on the one hand, the respective proportions of men in the workforce able to satisfy the requirement of two years' employment under the disputed rule and of those unable to do so, and, on the other, to compare those proportions as regards women in the workforce. It is not sufficient to consider the number of persons affected, since that depends on the number of working people in the Member State as a whole as well as the percentages of men and women employed in that State.

* * *

63. In this case, it appears from the order for reference that in 1985, the year in which the requirement of two years' employment was introduced, 77.4% of men and 68.9% of women fulfilled that condition.

64. Such statistics do not appear, on the face of it, to show that a considerably smaller percentage of women than men is able to fulfil the requirement imposed by the disputed rule.

65. Accordingly, the answer to the third question must be that in order to establish whether a measure adopted by a Member State has disparate effect as between men and women to such a degree as to amount to indirect discrimination for the purposes of Article 119 of the Treaty, the national court must verify whether the statistics available indicate that a considerably smaller percentage of women than men is able to fulfil the requirement imposed by that measure. If that is the case, there is indirect sex discrimination, unless that measure is justified by objective factors unrelated to any discrimination based on sex.

QUESTION 5

66. By its fifth question the national court seeks to ascertain the legal criteria for establishing the objective justification, for the purposes of indirect discrimination under Article 119 of the Treaty, of a measure adopted by a Member State in pursuance of its social policy.

69. It is settled case-law that if a Member State is able to show that the measures chosen reflect a necessary aim of its social policy and are suitable and necessary for achieving that aim, the mere fact that the legislative provision affects far more women than men at work cannot be regarded as a breach of Article 119 of the Treaty (see, in particular, Case C–444/93 Megner and Scheffel v. Innungskrankenkasse Vorderpfalz [1995] ECR I–4741, paragraph 24, and Freers and Speckmann, cited above, paragraph 28).

70. In this case, the United Kingdom Government contends that the risk that the exposure of employers to proceedings for unfair dismissal brought by employees who had only fairly recently been engaged is a deterrent to recruitment, so that extension of the qualifying period for protection against dismissal would stimulate recruitment.

71. It cannot be disputed that the encouragement of recruitment constitutes a legitimate aim of social policy.

72. It must also be ascertained, in the light of all the relevant factors and taking into account the possibility of achieving the social policy aim in question by other means, whether such an aim appears to be unrelated to any discrimination based on sex and

whether the disputed rule, as a means to its achievement, is capable of advancing that aim.

73. In that connection, the United Kingdom Government maintains that a Member State should merely have to show that it was reasonably entitled to consider that the measure would advance a social policy aim. It relies to that end on Case C–317/93 Nolte [1995] ECR I–4625.

74. It is true that in paragraph 33 of the *Nolte* case the Court observed that, in choosing the measures capable of achieving the aims of their social and employment policy, the Member States have a broad margin of discretion.

75. However, although social policy is essentially a matter for the Member States under Community law as it stands, the fact remains that the broad margin of discretion available to the Member States in that connection cannot have the effect of frustrating the implementation of a fundamental principle of Community law such as that of equal pay for men and women.

76. Mere generalisations concerning the capacity of a specific measure to encourage recruitment are not enough to show that the aim of the disputed rule is unrelated to any discrimination based on sex nor to provide evidence on the basis of which it could reasonably be considered that the means chosen were suitable for achieving that aim.

77. Accordingly, the answer to the fifth question must be that if a considerably smaller percentage of women than men is capable of fulfilling the requirement of two years' employment imposed by the disputed rule, it is for the Member State, as the author of the allegedly discriminatory rule, to show that the said rule reflects a legitimate aim of its social policy, that that aim is unrelated to any discrimination based on sex, and that it could reasonably consider that the means chosen were suitable for attaining that aim.

Notes and Questions

1. **Effect of Later EU Directives?** Would the decision in *Bilka-Kaufhaus* be the same under EU Directive 97/80? Under Directive 2002/73?

2. **Rationale for Reaching Indirect Discrimination?** What is the rationale for banning indirect as well as direct discrimination? Is the justification the same as for the adoption of "disparate impact" analysis under Title VII?

3. **"Business Necessity"?** Is the employer's burden in an indirect discrimination case different from the employer's burden in a U.S. disparate impact case? Would the U.K.'s justification presented in

Regina v Secretary of State for Employment, be sufficient to overcome a prima facie case of disparate impact discrimination in the U.S?

D. COMPARABLE WORTH

Note: Article 119 of EEC Treaty and EEC Directive 75/117

The Treaty establishing what has become the European Union required member states to ensure "that the principle of equal pay for male and female workers for equal work or work of equal value is applied." Article 141 (originally Article. 119) of the Treaty Establishing the European Community. The Article defines "pay" as "the ordinary basic or minimum wage or salary and any other consideration, whether in cash or in kind, which the worker receives directly or indirectly, in respect of his employment, from his employer." It defines "equal pay without discrimination based on sex" as:

> (a) that pay for the same work at piece rates shall be calculated on the basis of the same unit of measurement;
>
> (b) that pay for work at time rates shall be the same for the same job.

An implementing directive, 75/117, provides in relevant part:

> Article 1
>
> The principle of equal pay for men and women outlined in Article 119 of the Treaty, hereinafter called "principle of equal pay", means, for the same work or for work to which equal value is attributed, the elimination of all discrimination on grounds of sex with regard to all aspects and conditions of remuneration.
>
> In particular, where a job classification system is used for determining pay, it must be based on the same criteria for both men and women and so drawn up as to exclude any discrimination on grounds of sex.
>
> Article 2
>
> Member States shall introduce into their national legal systems such measures as are necessary to enable all employees who consider themselves wronged by failure to apply the principle of equal pay to pursue their claims by judicial process after possible recourse to other competent authorities.
>
> Article 3
>
> Member States shall abolish all discrimination between men and women arising from laws, regulations or administrative provisions which is contrary to the principle of equal pay.

Article 4

Member States shall take the necessary measures to ensure that provisions appearing in collective agreements, wage scales, wage agreements or individual contracts of employment which are contrary to the principle of equal pay shall be, or may be declared, null and void or may be amended.

Article 5

Member States shall take the necessary measures to protect employees against dismissal by the employer as a reaction to a complaint within the undertaking or to any legal proceedings aimed at enforcing compliance with the principle of equal pay.

Article 6

Member States shall, in accordance with their national circumstances and legal systems, take the measures necessary to ensure that the principle of equal pay is applied. They shall see that effective means are available to take care that this principle is observed.

RUMMLER v DATO–DRUCK GmbH

[1987] ICR 774 (E.C.J.)

* * *

4. The plaintiff in the main proceedings, who is classified in Wage Group III, considers that she ought to be classified in Wage Group IV since she carries out work falling under that wage group; in particular, she is required to pack parcels weighing more than 20 kg, which for her represents heavy physical work.

5. The defendant in the main proceedings denies that the plaintiff's duties are of the nature described by her; it considers that they do not even fulfil the conditions for classification in Wage Group III, in which the plaintiff is now classified and that having regard to the nature of her duties, which make only slight muscular demands, she should be classified in Wage Group II.

7. By its first question the national court seeks to ascertain whether a job classification system based on the criteria of muscle demand or muscular effort and the heaviness of the work is compatible with the principle of equal pay for men and women.

8. According to Dato–Druck G.m.b.H., pay criteria must in essence be established in accordance with the duties actually performed, and not by reference to the personal attributes of the worker who carries them out. In its view, the criteria of muscle demand and the heaviness of the work are in no way discriminatory in so far as they correspond to the characteristics of the duties

performed and are used in a system which also refers to the criteria of ability, mental effort and responsibility.

11. In replying to question 1, reference must first be made to the general rule laid down by the first paragraph of article 1 of Council Directive (75/117/E.E.C.), which provides for the elimination of all discrimination on grounds of sex with regard to all aspects and conditions of remuneration for the same work or for work to which equal value is attributed.

12. That general rule is applied in the second paragraph of article 1, which provides that a job classification system:

> "... must be based on the same criteria for both men and women and so drawn up as to exclude any discrimination on grounds of sex."

13. It follows that the principle of equal pay requires essentially that the nature of the work to be carried out be considered objectively. Consequently, the same work or work to which equal value is attributed must be remunerated in the same manner whether it is carried out by a man or by a woman. Where a job classification system is used in determining remuneration, that system must be based on criteria which do not differ according to whether the work is carried out by a man or by a woman and must not be organised, as a whole, in such a manner that it has the practical effect of discriminating generally against workers of one sex.

14. Consequently, criteria corresponding to the duties performed meet the requirements of article 1 of the Directive where those duties by their nature require particular physical effort or are physically heavy. In differentiating rates of pay, it is consistent with the principle of nondiscrimination to use a criterion based on the objectively measurable expenditure of effort necessary in carrying out the work or the degree to which, reviewed objectively, the work is physically heavy.

15. Even where a particular criterion, such as that of demand on the muscles, may in fact tend to favour male workers, since it may be assumed that in general they are physically stronger than woman workers, it must, in order to determine whether or not it is discriminatory, be considered in the context of the whole job classification system, having regard to other criteria influencing rates of pay. A system is not necessarily discriminatory simply because one of its criteria makes reference to attributes more characteristic of men. In order for a job classification system as a whole to be non-discriminatory and thus to comply with the principles of the directive, it must, however, be established in such a manner that it includes, if the nature of the tasks in question so permits, jobs to which equal value is attributed and for which

regard is had to other criteria in relation to which women workers may have a particular aptitude.

16. It is for the national courts to determine on a case-by-case basis whether a job classification system as a whole allows proper account to be taken of the criteria necessary for adjusting pay rates according to the conditions required for the performance of the various duties throughout the undertaking.

17. * * * Council Directive (75/117/E.E.C.) of 10 February 1975 on the approximation of the laws of the member states relating to the application of the principle of equal pay for men and women does not prohibit the use, in a job classification system for the purpose of determining rates of pay, of the criterion of muscle demand or muscular effort or that of the heaviness of the work if, in view of the nature of the tasks involved, the work to be performed requires the use of a certain degree of physical strength, so long as the system as a whole, by taking into account other criteria, precludes any discrimination on grounds of sex.

18. [T]he national court wishes in substance to know whether, in the event that the criteria of muscle demand or muscular effort and of the heaviness of the work are compatible with Council Directive (75/117/E.E.C.), the fact that in determining to what extent work requires an effort or is demanding or heavy regard is had to the degree to which the work requires an effort or is demanding or heavy for women workers satisfies the requirements of the directive.

22. * * * [N]othing in the directive prevents the use in determining wage rates of a criterion based on the degree of muscular effort objectively required by a specific job or the objective degree of heaviness of the job.

23. The directive lays down the principle of equal pay for equal work. It follows that the work actually carried out must be remunerated in accordance with its nature. Any criterion based on values appropriate only to workers of one sex carries with it a risk of discrimination and may jeopardise the main objective of the directive, equal treatment for the same work. That is true even of a criterion based on values corresponding to the average performance of workers of the sex considered to have less natural ability for the purposes of that criterion, for the result would be another form of pay discrimination: work objectively requiring greater strength would be paid at the same rate as work requiring less strength.

24. The failure to take into consideration values corresponding to the average performance of female workers in establishing a progressive pay scale based on the degree of muscle demand and muscular effort may indeed have the effect of placing women workers, who cannot take jobs which are beyond their physical

strength, at a disadvantage. That difference in treatment may, however, be objectively justified by the nature of the job when such a difference is necessary in order to ensure a level of pay appropriate to the effort required by the work and thus corresponds to a real need on the part of the undertaking: see Bilka–Kaufhaus G.m.b.H v. Weber von Hartz (Case 170/94) [1987] I.C.R. 110. As has already been stated, however, a job classification system must, in so far as the nature of the tasks in question permits, include other criteria which serve to ensure that the system as a whole is not discriminatory.

25. [I]t follows from Council Directive (75/117/E.E.C.) that (a) the criteria governing pay-rate classification must ensure that work which is objectively the same attracts the same rate of pay whether it is performed by a man or a woman; (b) the use of values reflecting the average performance of workers of one sex as a basis for determining the extent to which work makes demands or requires effort or whether it is heavy constitutes a form of discrimination on grounds of sex, contrary to the directive; (c) in order for a job classification system not to be discriminatory as a whole, it must, in so far as the nature of the tasks carried out in the undertaking permits, take into account criteria for which workers of each sex may show particular aptitude.

PICKSTONE AND OTHERS v FREEMANS plc

[1988] 2 All ER 803, [1988] 3 WLR 265, [1989] A.C. 66 (H. L.)

Nicholls L.J. [opinions of other law lords are omitted]

The five applicants, Mrs. Pickstone and four of her female colleagues, are employed by Freemans Plc., a mail order company, as "warehouse operatives." They contend that their work is of equal value to that of a Mr. Phillips, who is employed by the employers as a "checker warehouse operative." They are not paid as much as he is. So they made a complaint to the industrial tribunal, sitting at Cambridge. Before that tribunal the employers contended that men as well as women were employed as warehouse operatives, and paid equally, and that men and women were also employed as checker warehouse operatives. The employers submitted that in those circumstances it was not open to the applicants as warehouse operatives, paid equally with their male colleagues, to claim equality of pay with Mr. Phillips, a checker warehouse operative. Issue was joined before the industrial tribunal on that submission of law, without the facts being investigated and without any formal admission by the applicants that there are male employees doing like work to them. Thus, in effect, the industrial tribunal heard and decided a preliminary question of law on assumed facts.

The applicants base their claims on section 1(2)(c) of the Equal Pay Act 1970 and also on article 119 of the E.E.C. Treaty.

Equal Pay Act 1970 Section 1(1) of the Equal Pay Act 1970 implies an equality clause into every contract of employment of a woman which does not already include such a clause. The nature and effect of an equality clause are set out in section 1(2). An equality clause has a similar effect in each of the three circumstances specified in paragraphs (a), (b) and (c) of section 1(2). Accordingly, for convenience I will omit sub-paragraphs (i) and (ii) from paragraphs (b) and (c) when setting out the material parts of section 1(2), as follows:

> "(2) An equality clause is a provision which relates to terms (whether concerned with pay or not) of a contract under which a woman is employed (the 'woman's contract'), and has the effect that—
>
> (a) where the woman is employed on like work with a man in the same employment—
>
> (i) if (apart from the equality clause) any term of the woman's contract is or becomes less favourable to the woman than a term of a similar kind in the contract under which that man is employed, that term of the woman's contract shall be treated as so modified as not to be less favourable, and
>
> (ii) if (apart from the equality clause) at any time the woman's contract does not include a term corresponding to a term benefiting that man included in the contract under which he is employed, the woman's contract shall be treated as including such a term;
>
> (b) where the woman is employed on work rated as equivalent with that of a man in the same employment—
>
> (i) . . . and
>
> (ii) . . .
>
> (c) where a woman is employed on work which, not being work in relation to which paragraph (a) or (b) above applies, is, in terms of the demands made on her (for instance under such headings as effort, skill and decision), of equal value to that of a man in the same employment—
>
> (i) . . . and
>
> (ii) . . ."

Like work under paragraph (a) means work of the same or of a broadly similar nature where any differences between what the woman does and what the man does are not of practical importance in relation to terms and conditions of employment. Work is only rated as equivalent under paragraph (b) if the woman's and the man's jobs have been rated as equivalent on a job evaluation study.

The employers' argument, which was accepted by the industrial tribunal and the appeal tribunal, is straightforward. Paragraph (c), expressly and unambiguously, does not apply where the woman is employed on work to which either paragraph (a) or paragraph (b) applies. Paragraph (c) applies only where the woman is employed on work "not being work in relation to which paragraph (a) or (b) above applies." Hence, it was submitted, if the woman is in fact employed on like work with a man (meaning any man) in the same employment, paragraph (a) applies to her case whether she likes it or not, and she is thereby excluded from the scope of paragraph (c). Likewise with paragraph (b).

The applicants' argument is that the exclusionary words in paragraph (c) "not being" are ambiguous, and that one of the possible meanings of the word "applies" is applies in the sense that the woman is not employed on like work with, or on work rated as equivalent with that of, a man in the same employment with whom the woman is comparing herself. It is for the applicant to choose the man with whose work she wishes to compare hers: Ainsworth v. Glass Tubes Components Ltd. [1977] I.C.R. 347, and Parliament, when adding paragraph (c) to section 1(2) in 1983, cannot have intended to go against that principle and compel a woman to compare herself with a man under paragraph (a). In the present case the applicants are doing what traditionally has been "women's work" and they should be free to have recourse for comparison to other work of equal value to theirs.

In reply Mr. Carr submitted that this construction is untenable. The scheme of the section is to imply an equality clause into the woman's contract, with immediate effect, viz., with effect from the inception of the woman's contract. Where a woman is employed on like work with a man, paragraph (a) applies automatically, with the consequential, immediate deemed modification of the relevant term in the woman's contract. Paragraph (a) applies in this way irrespective of whether any complaint is made to the industrial tribunal. Hence, if a complaint is made and is successful, the woman has a claim not merely for the future: she can claim arrears of remuneration or damages: section 2(1).

But, continued Mr. Carr's submission, Mr. Pannick's construction is inconsistent with this, because on Mr. Pannick's construction paragraph (a) would not apply (and, indeed, none of the paragraphs would apply) unless and until the woman selects a male comparable.

Argument was also addressed to us on the mischief which section 1(2)(c) was intended to cure. This requires a consideration of Community law, because it was in response to a decision of the European Court of Justice that section 1(2)(c) was added to the Equal Pay Act 1970.

COMMUNITY LAW: ARTICLE 119

The United Kingdom became a member of the European Economic Community on 1 January 1973, and the E.E.C. Treaty was introduced into English law by section 2 of the European Communities Act 1972.

Article 119 is in these terms:

> "Each member state shall during the first stage ensure and subsequently maintain the application of the principle that men and women should receive equal pay for equal work. For the purpose of this article, 'pay' means the ordinary basic or minimum wage or salary and any other consideration, whether in cash or in kind, which the worker receives, directly or indirectly, in respect of his employment for his employer. Equal pay without discrimination based on sex means: (a) that pay for the same work at piece rates shall be calculated on the basis of the same unit of measurement; (b) that pay for work at time rates shall be the same for the same job."

* * *

In 1975, concerned at the uneven progress being made by member states in implementation of article 119, the council of the European Communities adopted Council Directive (75/117/E.E.C.), which it will be convenient to call "the equal pay directive." The material parts of that Directive read:

* * *

"ARTICLE 1.

> "The principle of equal pay for men and women outlined in article 119 of the Treaty, hereafter called 'principle of equal pay,' means, for the same work or for work to which equal value is attributed, the elimination of all discrimination on grounds of sex with regard to all aspects and conditions of remuneration. In particular, where a job classification is used for determining pay, it must be based on the same criteria for both men and women and so drawn up as to exclude any discrimination on grounds of sex.

"ARTICLE 2.

> "Member states shall introduce into their national legal systems such measures as are necessary to enable all employees who consider themselves wronged by failure to apply the

principle of equal pay to pursue their claims by judicial process after possible recourse to other competent authorities . . .

"ARTICLE 4.

"Member states shall take the necessary measures to ensure that provisions appearing in collective agreements, wage scales, wage agreements or individual contracts of employment which are contrary to the principle of equal pay shall be, or may be declared, null and void or may be amended."

* * *

In this court Mr. Pannick submitted that the principle of equal pay for equal work enunciated in article 119, as re-stated or clarified in article 1 of the equal pay directive, entitles men and women to equal pay for the same work and (likewise) to equal pay for work to which equal value is attributed. They are entitled to equal pay in both those instances, and their entitlement to equal pay for work of equal value is not dependent upon there being no person of the other sex currently engaged in the same work as the person making the claim. If there is a man, or if there are men, doing the same work but being paid no more than the woman, that will be evidence, whose weight will depend upon all the circumstances, that the payment of a higher wage to other men who are doing work which is different but of no greater value is due to a material factor other than the difference in sex.

The argument in favour of the narrower construction of article 119 is that it makes sense for recourse not to be had to the less precise and much more difficult yardstick of work of "equal value" when there is to hand the more precise and less controversial one of "same work." The second limb of article 1 of the equal pay directive (work to which equal value is to be attributed), preceded as it is by the disjunctive "or," is applicable only when the first limb (same work) is not in point. If the first limb is applicable, so that there is a man doing the same work as the woman, but the woman is entitled nonetheless to compare herself to another man and his work she would, as the industrial tribunal said in this case, "have wandered into the territory of job evaluation." The principle of equal pay for men and women doing equal work is intended to avoid discrimination on the ground of sex, not to have effect on disputed differentials unrelated to sex. * * *

In my view Mr. Pannick's submission, in support of the first of these two interpretations of article 119, is correct. Article 119 enshrines a broad, general principle: equal pay for equal work. The equal pay directive makes clear that in this context equal work embraces work of equal value as well as work which is the same. I can see no justification for implying into this general principle, whereunder equal work includes both these categories, a rigid and inflexible limitation, to the effect that, although a woman is entitled to compare herself with a man doing work of equal value, she is only so entitled if and so long as no man is doing the same work as herself, and that whenever and for so long as there is a man doing the same work the woman cannot make that comparison, even if the difference in pay is attributable solely to grounds of sex. It makes the presence per se of one man doing the same work, which in some cases might be wholly fortuitous or even, possibly, a situation contrived by an unscrupulous employer, a decisive factor, regardless of all the other circumstances of the case.

* * *

Thus "equal work" involves a comparison between the work (the nature of the services) performed by the woman and the work done by the man, and in making that comparison it is not essential that the man is still doing that work or that he was ever doing it at the same time as the woman. Absence of contemporaneity does not prevent the comparison being made, although such absence is material when considering, as a question of fact, whether the reason for the difference in pay is discrimination on grounds of sex. I do not see how this interpretation of article 119 permits of the conclusion that nonetheless contemporaneity is of the essence in relation to work of equal value, in that a woman is entitled to equality of pay with a man whose work is of equal value but only so long as contemporaneously there is no man doing the same work as herself.

* * *

Accordingly, for the reasons given, for my part I would allow the appeal and direct that these applications proceed in front of the industrial tribunal on the footing that under article 119, although not under section 1(2)(c) of the Equal Pay Act 1970, a woman employed on work which is the same as that of one man but which is also of equal value with the work of another man is not debarred from claiming equal pay with that other man by reason of the fact that she is already being paid as much as the man engaged on the same work as herself. In determining whether the work of these applicants is of equal value to that of the checker warehouse operatives, and in determining whether (to adopt and adapt the language of the European Court in Macarthys' case [1981] Q.B. 180, 198) the difference in pay between the warehouse operatives and the checker warehouse operatives is explicable by the operation of factors which are unconnected with any discrimination on grounds of sex, the industrial tribunal should give such weight to the factor that there is a man, or there are men, doing the same work as the applicants and being paid no more, as is appropriate having regard to all the circumstances. These are determinations of fact.

ENDERBY v FRENCHAY HEALTH AUTHORITY AND ANOTHER

[1994] ICR 112 (E.C.J.)

3. The applicant, who is employed as a speech therapist by the health authority, considers that she is a victim of sex discrimination due to the fact that at her level of seniority within the National Health Service, namely, chief 3, members of her profession, which is overwhelmingly a female profession, are appreciably less well paid than members of comparable professions in which, at an equivalent professional level, there are more men than women. In 1986, she brought proceedings against her employer before an industrial tribunal, claiming that her annual pay was only £10,106 while that of a principal clinical psychologist and of a grade 3 principal pharmacist, jobs which were of equal value to hers, was £12,527 and £14,106 respectively.

4. The applicant's claim was dismissed by the industrial tribunal and then, on appeal, by the appeal tribunal [1991] I.C.R. 382. The industrial tribunal considered that the differences in pay were the result of structures specific to each profession, and in particular the separate collective bargaining arrangements, which were not discriminatory. The appeal tribunal also considered that the differences were not attributable to discrimination. It held further that it had been established that the state of the employment market played some part in the difference in pay between speech therapists and pharmacists and that that was enough to justify the whole of the difference between those two professions.

* * *

7. In its first question, the Court of Appeal wishes to know whether the principle of equal pay for men and women requires the employer to prove, by providing objective justification, that a difference in pay between two jobs assumed to be of equal value, of which one is carried out almost exclusively by women and the other predominantly by men, does not constitute sex discrimination.

13. It is normally for the person alleging facts in support of a claim to adduce proof of such facts. Thus, in principle, the burden of proving the existence of sex discrimination as to pay lies with the worker who, believing himself to be the victim of such discrimination, brings legal proceedings against his employer with a view to removing the discrimination.

14. However, it is clear from the case law of the court that the onus may shift when that is necessary to avoid depriving workers who appear to be the victims of discrimination of any effective means of enforcing the principle of equal pay. Accordingly, when a measure distinguishing between employees on the basis of their hours of work has in practice an adverse impact on substantially more members of one or other sex, that measure must be regarded as contrary to the objective pursued by article 119 of the Treaty, unless the employer shows that it is based on objectively justified factors unrelated to any discrimination on grounds of sex: see Bilka–Kaufhaus G.m.b.H. v. Weber von Hartz (Case 170/84) [1987] I.C.R. 110, 125, para. 31; Kowalska v. Freie und Hansestadt Hamburg (Case C–33/89) [1992] I.C.R. 29, 35, para. 16 and Nimz v. Freie und Hansestadt Hamburg (Case C–184/89) [1991] E.C.R. I–297, 320, para. 15. Similarly, where an undertaking applies a system of pay which is wholly lacking in transparency, it is for the employer to prove that his practice in the matter of wages is not discriminatory, if a female worker establishes, in relation to a relatively large number of employees, that the average pay for women is less than that for men: see Handels-og Kontorfunktionaerernes Forbund i Danmark v. Dansk Arbejdsgiverforening (Case 109/88) [1991] I.C.R. 74, 80, para. 16.

15. In this case, as both the health authority and the United Kingdom observe, the circumstances are not exactly the same as in the cases just mentioned. First, it is not a question of de facto discrimination arising from a particular sort of arrangement such as may apply, for example, in the case of part-time workers. Secondly, there can be no complaint that the employer has applied a system of pay wholly lacking in transparency since the rates of pay of National Health Service speech therapists and pharmacists are decided by regular collective bargaining processes in which there is no evidence of discrimination as regards either of those two professions.

16. However, if the pay of speech therapists is significantly lower than that of pharmacists and if the former are almost exclusively women while the latter are predominantly men, there is a prima facie case of sex discrimination, at least where the two jobs in question are of equal value and the statistics describing that situation are valid.

17. It is for the national court to assess whether it may take into account those statistics, that is to say, whether they cover enough individuals, whether they illustrate purely fortuitous or short term phenomena, and whether, in general, they appear to be significant.

18. Where there is a prima facie case of discrimination, it is for the employer to show that there are objective reasons for the difference in pay. Workers would be unable to enforce the principle of equal pay before national courts if evidence of a prima facie case of discrimination did not shift to the employer the onus of showing that the pay differential is not in fact discriminatory: see, by analogy, Handels-og Kontorfunktionaerernes Forbund i Danmark v. Dansk Arbejdsgiverforening (Case 109/88) [1991] I.C.R. 74, 79, para. 13.

19. In these circumstances, the answer to the first question is that, where significant statistics disclose an appreciable difference in pay between two jobs of equal value, one of which is carried out almost exclusively by women and the other predominantly by men, article 119 of the Treaty requires the employer to show that that difference is based on objectively justified factors unrelated to any discrimination on grounds of sex.

20. In its second question, the Court of Appeal wishes to know whether the employer can rely as sufficient justification for the difference in pay upon the fact that the rates of pay of the jobs in question were decided by collective bargaining processes which, although carried out by the same parties, are distinct and which, considered separately, have no discriminatory effect.

* * *

22. The fact that the rates of pay at issue are decided by collective bargaining processes conducted separately for each of the two professional groups concerned, without any discriminatory effect within each group, does not preclude a finding of prima facie discrimination where the results of those processes show that two groups with the same employer and the same trade union are treated differently. If the employer could rely on the absence of discrimination within each of the collective bargaining processes taken separately as sufficient justification for the difference in pay, he could, as the German Government pointed out, easily circumvent the principle of equal pay by using * * * separate bargaining processes.

* * *

24. In its third question, the Court of Appeal wishes to know to what extent—wholly, in part or not at all—the fact that part of the difference in pay is attributable to a shortage of candidates for one job and to the need to attract them by higher salaries can objectively justify that pay differential.

* * *

26. The state of the employment market, which may lead an employer to increase the pay of a particular job in order to attract candidates, may constitute an objectively justified economic ground within the meaning of the case law cited above. How it is to be applied in the circumstances of each case depends on the facts and so falls within the jurisdiction of the national court.

27. If, as the question referred seems to suggest, the national court has been able to determine precisely what proportion of the increase in pay is attributable to market forces, it must necessarily accept that the pay differential is objectively justified to the extent of that proportion. When national authorities have to apply Community law, they must apply the principle of proportionality.

28. If that is not the case, it is for the national court to assess whether the role of market forces in determining the rate of pay was sufficiently significant to provide objective justification for part or all of the difference.

Notes and Questions

1. **Proof of Comparable Worth?** Is it practically possible to compare the value of different jobs? How should the court proceed in this area where the claimed disparity is not revealed in the employer's evaluation of its pay system?

2. **Judicial Legislation?** Consider the court's reasoning. Was comparable worth authorized by Community law?

3. **Market-Based Differential Defense?** If market forces are themselves the result of sex discrimination, do they nonetheless constitute a defense to a comparable worth claim?

E. AFFIRMATIVE ACTION (POSITIVE DISCRIMINATION)

In Europe affirmative action is referred to as "positive action." As in the United States, courts and legislatures have shown ambivalence over both the objectives and means employed in affirmative action arrangements. Nevertheless, in some situations the law allows its use.

ECKHARD KALANKE v FREIE HANSESTADT BREMEN

[1995] ECR I–3051

3. Paragraph 4 of the Landesgleichstellungsgesetz of 20 November 1990 (Bremen Law on Equal Treatment for Men and Women in the Public Service, Bremisches Gesetzblatt, p. 433, hereinafter 'the LGG') provides:

'Appointment, assignment to an official post and promotion

(1) In the case of an appointment (including establishment as a civil servant or judge) which is not made for training purposes, women who have the same qualifications as men applying for the same post are to be given priority in sectors where they are under-represented.

(2) In the case of an assignment to a position in a higher pay, remuneration and salary bracket, women who have the same qualifications as men applying for the same post are to be given priority if they are under-represented. This also applies in the case of assignment to a different official post and promotion.

* * *

(4) Qualifications are to be evaluated exclusively in accordance with the requirements of the occupation, post to be filled or career bracket. Specific experience and capabilities, such as those acquired as a result of family work, social commitment or unpaid activity, are part of the qualifications within the meaning of subparagraphs (1) and (2) if they are of use in performing the duties of the position in question.

(5) There is under-representation if women do not make up at least half of the staff in the individual pay, remuneration and salary brackets in the relevant personnel group within a department. This also applies to the function levels provided for in the organization chart.'

4. It appears from the order for reference that, at the final stage of recruitment to a post of Section Manager in the Bremen Parks Department, two candidates, both in BAT pay bracket III, were shortlisted:

— Mr. Kalanke, the plaintiff in the main proceedings, holder of a diploma in horticulture and landscape gardening, who had worked since 1973 as a horticultural employee in the Parks Department and acted as permanent assistant to the Section Manager and

— Ms. Glissmann, holder of a diploma in landscape gardening since 1983 and also employed, since 1975, as a horticultural employee in the Parks Department.

5. The Staff Committee refused to give its consent to Mr. Kalanke' s promotion, proposed by the Parks Department management. Reference to arbitration resulted in a recommendation in favour of Mr. Kalanke. The Staff Committee then stated that the arbitration had failed and appealed to the conciliation board which,

in a decision binding on the employer, considered that the two candidates were equally qualified and that priority should therefore be given, in accordance with the LGG, to the woman.

[T]he Bundesarbeitsgericht has stayed the proceedings and sought a preliminary ruling from the Court * * * [.]

15. The purpose of the Directive is, as stated in Article 1(1), to put into effect in the Member States the principle of equal treatment for men and women as regards, inter alia, access to employment, including promotion. Article 2(1) states that the principle of equal treatment means that 'there shall be no discrimination whatsoever on grounds of sex either directly or indirectly'.

16. A national rule that, where men and women who are candidates for the same promotion are equally qualified, women are automatically to be given priority in sectors where they are under-represented, involves discrimination on grounds of sex.

17. It must, however, be considered whether such a national rule is permissible under Article 2(4), which provides that the Directive 'shall be without prejudice to measures to promote equal opportunity for men and women, in particular by removing existing inequalities which affect women' s opportunities'.

18. That provision is specifically and exclusively designed to allow measures which, although discriminatory in appearance, are in fact intended to eliminate or reduce actual instances of inequality which may exist in the reality of social life (see Case 312/86 Commission v. France [1988] ECR 6315, paragraph 15).

19. It thus permits national measures relating to access to employment, including promotion, which give a specific advantage to women with a view to improving their ability to compete on the labour market and to pursue a career on an equal footing with men.

* * *

21. Nevertheless, as a derogation from an individual right laid down in the Directive, Article 2(4) must be interpreted strictly * * * ..

22. National rules which guarantee women absolute and unconditional priority for appointment or promotion go beyond promoting equal opportunities and overstep the limits of the exception in Article 2(4) of the Directive.

23. Furthermore, in so far as it seeks to achieve equal representation of men and women in all grades and levels within a department, such a system substitutes for equality of opportunity as envisaged in Article 2(4) the result which is only to be arrived at by providing such equality of opportunity.

24. The answer to the national court' s questions must therefore be that Article 2(1) and (4) of the Directive precludes national rules such as those in the present case which, where candidates of different sexes shortlisted for promotion are equally qualified, automatically give priority to women in sectors where they are under-represented, under-representation being deemed to exist when women do not make up at least half of the staff in the individual pay brackets in the relevant personnel group or in the function levels provided for in the organization chart.

KATARINA ABRAHAMSSON AND LEIF ANDERSON v ELISABET FOGELQVIST

[2000] ECR I–5539 (E.C.J.)

5. Since the entry into force of the Treaty of Amsterdam on 1 May 1999, Article 141(1) and (4) EC provides:

> 1. Each Member State shall ensure that the principle of equal pay for male and female workers for equal work or work of equal value is applied.
>
> * * *
>
> 4. With a view to ensuring full equality in practice between men and women in working life, the principle of equal treatment shall not prevent any Member State from maintaining or adopting measures providing for specific advantages in order to make it easier for the under-represented sex to pursue a vocational activity or to prevent or compensate for disadvantages in professional careers.

6. Declaration No 28 concerning Article 141(4) (ex Article 119(4)) of the Treaty establishing the European Community, annexed to the final act of the Treaty of Amsterdam, states:

> When adopting measures referred to in Article 141(4) of the Treaty establishing the European Community, Member States should, in the first instance, aim at improving the situation of women in working life.

7. Point 2 of the second paragraph of Article 16 of the Jamstalldhetslagen (1991:433) (Swedish Law on equality) provides that positive discrimination measures are authorised where they contribute to efforts to promote equality in the workplace.

16. On 3 June 1996 the University of Goteborg announced a vacancy for the chair of Professor of Hydrospheric Sciences. The vacancy notice indicated that the appointment to that post should contribute to promotion of equality of the sexes in professional life and that positive discrimination might be applied * * *.

17. Eight candidates applied, including Ms. Abrahamsson, Ms. Destouni and Ms. Fogelqvist, and Mr. Anderson.

18. The appointments committee of the Faculty of Sciences (hereinafter the selection board) voted twice, on the first occasion in relation to the candidates' scientific qualifications. In that vote Mr. Anderson came first with five votes and Ms. Destouni received three votes. On the second vote, taking account both of scientific merits and of [regulations promoting positive discrimination], Ms. Destouni came first with six votes as compared with two for Mr. Anderson. The selection board proposed to the Rector of the University of Goteborg that Ms. Destouni be appointed * * *. Referring, in both cases, to experts' reports, the selection board placed Mr. Anderson second and Ms. Fogelqvist third.

19. After Ms. Destouni withdrew her application, the Rector of the University decided on 27 June 1997 to refer the matter back to the selection board for it to decide on the remaining applications in the light of equality between men and women * * * and the university's plan for equality between men and women. On 6 November 1997 the selection board stated that it could not re-examine the case having regard to those factors since the question of equality had already been taken into account in its first decision.

20. On 18 November 1997 the Rector of the University of Goteborg decided to appoint Ms. Fogelqvist to the professorial chair. In his decision, the Rector referred to * * * to the University's plan for equality between men and women and stated that the difference between the respective merits of Mr. Anderson and Ms. Fogelqvist was not so considerable that positive discrimination in favour of the latter constituted a breach of the requirement of objectivity in the making of appointments. * * *

* * *

43. [I]n its judgment in Case C–158/97 Badeck and Others [2000] ECR I–0000, paragraph 23, the Court held that a measure which is intended to give priority in promotion to women in sectors of the public service where they are under-represented must be regarded as compatible with Community law

> — where it does not automatically and unconditionally give priority to women when women and men are equally qualified, and
>
> — where the candidatures are the subject of an objective assessment which takes account of the specific personal situations of all candidates.

THE FIRST QUESTION

44. The issue raised by the first question is whether Article 2(1) and (4) precludes national legislation, such as the Swedish

legislation at issue in the main proceedings, under which a candidate for a public post who belongs to the under-represented sex and possesses sufficient qualifications for that post must be chosen in preference to a candidate of the opposite sex who would otherwise have been appointed, where this is necessary to secure the appointment of a candidate of the under-represented sex and the difference between the respective merits of the candidates is not so great as to give rise to a breach of the requirement of objectivity in making appointments.

* * *

47. In paragraphs 31 and 32 of *Badeck*, cited above, the Court held that it is legitimate for the purposes of that assessment for certain positive and negative criteria to be taken into account which, although formulated in terms which are neutral as regards sex and thus capable of benefiting men too, in general favour women. Thus, it may be decided that seniority, age and the date of last promotion are to be taken into account only in so far as they are of importance for the suitability, qualifications and professional capability of candidates. Similarly, it may be prescribed that the family status or income of the partner is immaterial and that part-time work, leave and delays in completing training as a result of looking after children or dependents in need of care must not have a negative effect.

* * *

50. As regards the selection procedure at issue in the main proceedings, it does not appear from the relevant Swedish legislation that assessment of the qualifications of candidates by reference to the requirements of the vacant post is based on clear and unambiguous criteria such as to prevent or compensate for disadvantages in the professional career of members of the under-represented sex.

51. On the contrary, under that legislation, a candidate for a public post belonging to the under-represented sex and possessing sufficient qualifications for that post must be chosen in preference to a candidate of the opposite sex who would otherwise have been appointed, where that measure is necessary for a candidate belonging to the under-represented sex to be appointed.

52. It follows that the legislation at issue in the main proceedings automatically grants preference to candidates belonging to the under-represented sex, provided that they are sufficiently qualified, subject only to the proviso that the difference between the merits of the candidates of each sex is not so great as to result in a breach of the requirement of objectivity in making appointments.

53. The scope and effect of that condition cannot be precisely determined, with the result that the selection of a candidate from among those who are sufficiently qualified is ultimately based on the mere fact of belonging to the under-represented sex, and that this is so even if the merits of the candidate so selected are inferior to those of a candidate of the opposite sex. Moreover, candidatures are not subjected to an objective assessment taking account of the specific personal situations of all the candidates. It follows that such a method of selection is not such as to be permitted by Article 2(4) of the Directive.

54. In those circumstances, it is necessary to determine whether legislation such as that at issue in the main proceedings is justified by Article 141(4) EC.

55. In that connection, it is enough to point out that, even though Article 141(4) EC allows the Member States to maintain or adopt measures providing for special advantages intended to prevent or compensate for disadvantages in professional careers in order to ensure full equality between men and women in professional life, it cannot be inferred from this that it allows a selection method of the kind at issue in the main proceedings which appears, on any view, to be disproportionate to the aim pursued.

56. The answer to the first question must therefore be that Article 2(1) and (4) of the Directive and Article 141(4) EC preclude national legislation under which a candidate for a public post who belongs to the under-represented sex and possesses sufficient qualifications for that post must be chosen in preference to a candidate of the opposite sex who would otherwise have been appointed, where this is necessary to secure the appointment of a candidate of the under-represented sex and the difference between the respective merits of the candidates is not so great as to give rise to a breach of the requirement of objectivity in making appointments.

* * *

THE THIRD QUESTION

60. By its third question, the national court seeks to ascertain whether Article 2(1) and (4) of the Directive precludes a rule of national case-law under which a candidate belonging to the under-represented sex may be granted preference over a competitor of the opposite sex provided that the candidates possess equivalent or substantially equivalent merits.

61. On that point, it is enough to say that, as indicated in paragraph 43 above, such a rule must be regarded as compatible with Community law where the candidatures are subjected to an objective assessment which takes account of the specific personal situations of all the candidates.

Note: Recent EU Directives Concerning Positive Action

The most recent EU directives on employment discrimination address positive action. For example, Directive 2002/73 explains in its preamble:

> (14) Member States may, under Article 141(4) of the Treaty, maintain or adopt measures providing for specific advantages, in order to make it easier for the underrepresented sex to pursue a vocational activity or to prevent or compensate for disadvantages in professional careers. Given the current situation, and bearing in mind Declaration No 28 to the Amsterdam Treaty, Members States should, in the first instance, aim at improving the situation of women in working life.
>
> (15) The prohibition of discrimination should be without prejudice to the maintenance or adoption of measures intended to prevent or compensate for disadvantages suffered by a group of persons of one sex. Such measures permit organisations of persons of one sex where their main object is the promotion of the special needs of those persons and the promotion of equality between women and men.

Amended Article 2 now includes this provision:

> 8. Member States may maintain or adopt measures within the meaning of Article 141(4) of the Treaty with a view to ensuring full equality in practice between men and women.

The language of the race discrimination directive, 2000/43, differs:

> With a view to ensuring full equality in practice, the principle of equal treatment shall not prevent any Member State from maintaining or adopting specific measures to prevent or compensate for disadvantages linked to racial or ethnic origin.

Similarly, the Framework Directive, 2000/78, provides:

> 1. With a view to ensuring full equality in practice, the principle of equal treatment shall not prevent any Member State from maintaining or adopting specific measures to prevent or compensate for disadvantages linked to any of the grounds referred to in Article 1.
>
> 2. With regard to disabled persons, the principle of equal treatment shall be without prejudice to the right of Member States to maintain or adopt provisions on the protection of health and safety at work or to measures aimed at creating or maintaining provisions or facilities for safeguarding or promoting their integration into the working environment.

Notes and Questions

1. **Effect of Later Directives?** Do the more recent directives change the law as set forth in *Kalanke* and *Abrahamsson*?

2. **Goals vs. Quotas?** Has the EU embraced a distinction between goals and quotas? Why does the court in *Abrahamsson* give such weight to relative qualification?

3. **Standard of Judicial Review?** What is the standard of review of positive action programs in the EU?

4. **South Africa**. Section 9 of South Africa's Constitution provides:

> 9. Equality
>
> (1) Everyone is equal before the law and has the right to equal protection and benefit of the law.
>
> (2) Equality includes the full and equal enjoyment of all rights and freedoms. To promote the achievement of equality, legislative and other measures designed to protect or advance persons, or categories of persons, disadvantaged by unfair discrimination may be taken. (3) The state may not unfairly discriminate directly or indirectly against anyone on one or more grounds, including race, gender, sex, pregnancy, marital status, ethnic or social origin, colour, sexual orientation, age, disability, religion, conscience, belief, culture, language and birth. * * *
>
> (5) Discrimination on one or more of the grounds listed in subsection (3) is unfair unless it is established that the discrimination is fair.

South Afr. Const. 1996, §§ 9(1) and 9(2) (available at http://www.acts.co.za/constitution/index.ht).

Note: Ev Chinnaiah v. State of Andhra Pradesh [2004] 4 LRI 705 (India)

India's constitution, effective in 1950, not only provides for the possibility of affirmative action, but embodies the expectation that such programs will occur. Unlike the United States, its deep social and economic divisions trace not to slavery but to a rigid and complex Hindu caste system, imposed at birth according to the family's traditional occupation, and reinforced by British colonial rule. The system included four castes arranged in a hierarchy from priests and the educated elite at the top to peasants and workers at the bottom. Outcasts, or untouchables, were outside the caste system entirely. In addition to abolishing untouchability and generally guaranteeing equality on grounds including race, religion, caste, and sex, India's Constitution provides for "reservations" of government employment positions and other opportunities, such as university student slots, for members of indigenous "scheduled tribes," and of the former untouchables, labeled "scheduled castes." A 1951 amendment empowered the government to make any "special provision for the advancement of any socially and educationally backward classes of citizens or for the scheduled castes and the scheduled tribes."

In response to the mandate to identify other backward classes, in addition to the former untouchables, a first Backward Classes Commission produced a report in 1955 identifying thousands of different groups as "backward" and recommending a range of reservations for government jobs and university slots. The Indian Parliament rejected the report and it was never implemented, although certain states took affirmative action measures. A 1963 Supreme Court decision held that total reservations could not exceed 50%. A second Backward Classes Commission produced another report in 1980, which the government ignored for ten years. The government's announcement in 1990 that it would implement the recommended reservations in government employment "provoked a torrent of criticism and an orgy of anti-reservation violence that included burning buses, trains and government buildings, blocking road and rail traffic, police firings, and as many as 100 suicides. The army was called out in several states to restore peace and order. The epicenter of the turbulence was New Delhi, the nation's capital, and spread throughout northern India." George H. Gadbois, Jr., International Insight: Mandal And The Other Backward Classes: Affirmative Action In India In The 1990s, 1 J.L. & Soc. Challenges 71, 74 (1997).

In 1992, the Indian Supreme Court issued a 900+ page decision *in Indra Sawhney v. Union of India*, (1992) 3 S.C.C. 212, in which it in large part upheld the government's adoption of the Commission's recommendations, with several modifications. It affirmed the 50% limit on total reservations (to be comprised of 22.5% for scheduled castes and tribes combined with 27% for other backward classes (OBCs) designated by the commission). It disagreed with a state government proposal to give preference to poorer sections of the OBCs, instead charging the national government with dividing the entire class of OBCs into "more backward" and "backward" categories and assigning a separate quota for each. It introduced the concept of a "creamy layer" (or most advanced segment of each class designated as backward) and required the government to create criteria for eliminating these segments from the set-asides. Additionally, the Court held that the reservations should apply only to hiring, and that promotions must be allocated according to merit independent of class designation.*

* The descriptions of South African and Indian law are from Brian Landsberg & Leslie Jacobs, Global Issues in Constitutional Law 95–97 (2007).

Chapter Four

REMEDIES AND ENFORCEMENT MECHANISMS

The effectiveness of the non-discrimination guarantee depends upon the remedial regime. What remedies are available? Declaratory relief? Individual injunctive relief? Systemic injunctive relief? Back pay? Compensatory damages? Punitive damages? Fines? Criminal sanctions? What is the enforcement mechanism? Private suit? Administrative hearings? Suit by government agency? Standing doctrine may either limit or encourage litigation.

One critic argues that in the U.K. and Europe, "remedies are limited by their focus on the individual. Instead of engaging actively in forward-looking reform of the kind essential to achieve comprehensive restructuring, the primary remedy available to tribunal is in the form of monetary compensation." Sandra Fredman, Discrimination Law 170, 172 (2002). She criticizes the lack of injunctive power in the English employment tribunals and also notes the "intense ambivalence to the function of compensation. Is it deterrent, or compensatory, or both?"

We begin first with a discussion of European and U.K. law on the obligation of member states to provide adequate remediation for violations of anti-discrimination provisions; and then turn to a comparison of enforcement mechanisms and remedies across a number of countries.

A. THE DUTY TO PROVIDE REMEDIATION

PRESTCOLD LTD. v IRVINE

[1981] ICR 777 (C.A.)

Fox L.J.

Mrs. Irvine was employed by the employers as a part-time audio secretary to the service administration manager. In 1976 the holder of the latter post, Mr. Rastell, was promoted. Mrs. Irvine had been helping him to a considerable extent; in practical terms she was the assistant service administration manager. She applied for the post when Mr. Rastell was promoted but a Mr. Dennahey was appointed. She continued in her job under Mr. Dennahey. Early in 1978 he decided to leave. Mrs. Irvine again applied for the job and was again unsuccessful. A Mr. Gorringe was appointed. Mr. Gorringe was 67 years of age; he was already in the employment of the employers.

Mrs. Irvine complained to the industrial tribunal that she had been discriminated against on the ground of her sex. The industrial tribunal decided, by a majority, that there was no discrimination when Mr. Dennahey was appointed but that there was discrimination when Mr. Gorringe was appointed. The tribunal found that there had been a failure to assess her qualities and that the employers had decided against her because she was a woman. There was no appeal against either of those findings. That brings me to the relief granted by the tribunal.

Section 65 of the Sex Discrimination Act 1975 is in the following terms:

> "(1) Where an industrial tribunal finds that a complaint presented to it under section 63 is well-founded the tribunal shall make such of the following as it considers just and equitable—
>
> (a) an order declaring the rights of the complainant and the respondent in relation to the act to which the complaint relates;
>
> (b) an order requiring the respondent to pay to the complainant compensation of an amount corresponding to any damages he could have been ordered by a county court or by a sheriff court to pay to the complainant if the complaint had fallen to be dealt with under section 66;
>
> (c) a recommendation that the respondent take within a specified period action appearing to the tribunal to be practicable for the purpose of obviating or reducing the

adverse effect on the complainant of any act of discrimination to which the complaint relates.

(2) The amount of compensation awarded to a person under subsection (1) (b) shall not exceed the amount for the time being specified in paragraph 20 (1) (b) of Schedule 1 to the Trade Union and Labour Relations Act 1974.

(3) If without reasonable justification the respondent to a complaint fails to comply with a recommendation made by an industrial tribunal under subsection (1) (c), then, if they think it just and equitable to do so—

(a) the tribunal may increase the amount of compensation required to be paid to the complainant in respect of the complaint by an order made under subsection (1) (b), or

(b) if an order under subsection (1) (b) could have been made but was not, the tribunal may make such an order."

Section 66 provides:

"(1) A claim by any person ('the claimant') that another person ('the respondent')—

(a) has committed an act of discrimination against the claimant which is unlawful by virtue of Part III, or

(b) is by virtue of section 41 or 42 to be treated as having committed such an act of discrimination against the claimant, may be made the subject of civil proceedings in like manner as any other claim in tort or (in Scotland) in reparation for breach of statutory duty."

The industrial tribunal awarded Mrs. Irvine the net amount of the difference up to the date of the hearing between the salary she was receiving and the salary being paid to Mr. Gorringe as the service administration manager. They also considered that there should be an award in respect of future loss. They therefore awarded a further sum covering the four months after the date of their decision at the same rate as for the period up to the date of the decision. The tribunal did not explain how they arrived at the four months. But there was no appeal or cross-appeal in respect of that period. I should add that it was contended before the Employment Appeal Tribunal that the industrial tribunal were wrong in treating Mr. Gorringe's salary as that which it could properly be assumed that Mrs. Irvine would have received if she had been appointed. The appeal tribunal indicated that they would have been obliged to remit that matter to the industrial tribunal but for the fact that the parties had been able to agree upon a figure.

The industrial tribunal, having dealt with the question of compensation in the manner which I have indicated, went on to make a recommendation, by a majority, in the following terms:

> "That the applicant be seriously considered as the most suitable candidate for the position of service administration manager as soon as it falls vacant, and that she be given opportunities for career development meanwhile, and that in the alternative she should continue to receive the difference in salary referred to above until she has been promoted either to that job or to a job of equivalent status."

* * *

[T]he appeal tribunal were of opinion that the intention of the legislature was that loss of wages should be dealt with under section 65 (1) (b) and not under (c):

> "It seems to us that it is not the intention that a tribunal should have power to make a recommendation that wages should be paid which, if not observed, would lead to an application for further compensation under section 65 (3)."

* * *

I should mention that Mrs. Irvine was, in fact, appointed to the post of service administration manager about a month after the hearing before the appeal tribunal. The dispute, therefore, relates to a limited period only.

* * *

In approaching the construction of section 65 (1) (c) it is to be borne in mind that it is not necessary for the protection of the complainant that the power conferred by paragraph (c) to make recommendations should extend to the remuneration to be paid to an employee. Paragraph (b) confers upon the tribunal power to order the employer to pay compensation for the discrimination complained of. It seems to me, therefore, that monetary compensation for loss of remuneration is fully provided for by paragraph (b).

If paragraph (c) authorises recommendations as to wages, the amount might exceed the limit on compensation provided by section 65 (2) as amended. While it is true that the employer would not be obliged to pay the wages and that, if he did not, the employee could only return to the tribunal and ask for compensation under (*b*) (which is subject to the limit), I do not think that such a position was contemplated by Parliament at all. I think that monetary compensation is dealt with by (b).

When one comes to the language of paragraph (c) itself, I do not think that it is at all apt to cover recommendations as to payment of remuneration. The paragraph authorises the making of "a recommendation that the respondent take within a specified period action appearing to the tribunal to be practicable." The paragraph is, therefore, concerned with the taking of some action "within a specified period." It is, I think, concerned with the taking of action without undue delay; an example is that given by the appeal tribunal, namely, the provision of training facilities within a specified period. It seems to me that the words "within a specified period" are inapt to cover a recommendation as to the payment of a particular remuneration during a period which might well extend over several years and even (if, for example, the position in question did not become vacant) over the whole of the employee's future period of employment by the employer. I am not saying that the taking of action may not extend over a substantial period but only that the payment of remuneration for employment does not, as a matter of the ordinary use of English, fit the description "take within a specified period action . . ." Accordingly, I think that the appeal tribunal reached the correct conclusion as to the ambit of paragraph (c) in section 65 (1).

MARSHALL v SOUTHAMPTON AND SOUTH–WEST HAMPSHIRE AREA HEALTH AUTHORITY

[1993] ECR I–4367 (E.C.J.)

2. Those questions [referred by the House of Lords] were raised in connection with a dispute between Miss Marshall and her former employer, Southampton and South West Hampshire Area Health Authority (hereinafter "the Authority"), concerning a claim for compensation for damage sustained by Miss Marshall as a result of her dismissal by the Authority.

* * *

4. The dispute in the main proceedings arises because the Industrial Tribunal, to which the Court of Appeal remitted the case to consider the question of compensation, assessed Miss Marshall' s financial loss at £18,405, including £7,710 by way of interest, and awarded her compensation of £19,405, including a sum of £1,000 compensation for injury to feelings.

5. It appears from the case-file that, according to section 65(1)(b) of the Sex Discrimination Act 1975 ("the SDA"), where an Industrial Tribunal finds that a complaint of unlawful sex discrimination in relation to employment is well founded, it shall, if it considers it just and equitable to do so, make an order requiring the respondent to pay to the complainant compensation of an amount corresponding to any damages he could have been ordered by a County Court to pay to the complainant. Under section 65(2) of the

SDA, however, the amount of compensation awarded may not exceed a specified limit, which at the relevant time was £6,250.

6. It also appears from the case-file that at that time an Industrial Tribunal had no power—or at least that the relevant provisions were ambiguous as to whether it had such a power—to award interest on compensation for an act of unlawful sex discrimination in relation to employment.

7. The Industrial Tribunal held that section 35A of the Supreme Court Act 1981 entitled it to include in its award a sum in respect of interest. In its view, compensation was the only appropriate remedy in Miss Marshall's case, but the limit laid down by section 65(2) of the SDA rendered that compensation inadequate and in breach of Article 6 of the Directive.

8. Following the Industrial Tribunal's decision, the Authority paid Miss Marshall the sum of £5,445 in addition to the £6,250 corresponding to the abovementioned statutory limit which it had paid even before the case had been remitted to the Industrial Tribunal. However, it appealed against the inclusion in the award of £7,710 in respect of interest.

* * *

Scope of the questions

11. In essence, the questions put by the House of Lords ask whether it follows from [Council Directive 76/207/EEC of 9 February 1976] that a victim of sex discrimination on the part of an authority which is an emanation of the State is entitled to full reparation for the loss and damage he or she has sustained and whether Article 6 of the Directive enables such a person to contest the applicability of national legislation which is intended to give effect to the Directive but sets limits to the compensation recoverable. The fundamental problem is therefore to determine the meaning and scope of Article 6 having regard to the principles and aims of the Directive.

* * *

Meaning and scope of Article 6 of Directive 76/207

* * *

19. The purpose of the Directive is to put into effect in the Member States the principle of equal treatment for men and women as regards the various aspects of employment, in particular working conditions, including the conditions governing dismissal.

* * *

22. Article 6 of the Directive puts Member States under a duty to take the necessary measures to enable all persons who consider themselves wronged by discrimination to pursue their claims by judicial process. Such obligation implies that the measures in question should be sufficiently effective to achieve the objective of the Directive and should be capable of being effectively relied upon by the persons concerned before national courts.

23. As the Court held in the judgment in Case 14/83 Von Colson and Kamann v. Land Nordrhein–Westfalen [1984] ECR 1891, at paragraph 18, Article 6 does not prescribe a specific measure to be taken in the event of a breach of the prohibition of discrimination, but leaves Member States free to choose between the different solutions suitable for achieving the objective of the Directive, depending on the different situations which may arise.

24. However, the objective is to arrive at real equality of opportunity and cannot therefore be attained in the absence of measures appropriate to restore such equality when it has not been observed. As the Court stated in paragraph 23 of the judgment in *Von Colson and Kamann*, cited above, those measures must be such as to guarantee real and effective judicial protection and have a real deterrent effect on the employer.

25. Such requirements necessarily entail that the particular circumstances of each breach of the principle of equal treatment should be taken into account. In the event of discriminatory dismissal contrary to Article 5(1) of the Directive, a situation of equality could not be restored without either reinstating the victim of discrimination or, in the alternative, granting financial compensation for the loss and damage sustained.

26. Where financial compensation is the measure adopted in order to achieve the objective indicated above, it must be adequate, in that it must enable the loss and damage actually sustained as a result of the discriminatory dismissal to be made good in full in accordance with the applicable national rules.

THE FIRST AND SECOND QUESTIONS

27. In its first question, the House of Lords seeks to establish whether it is contrary to Article 6 of the Directive for national provisions to lay down an upper limit on the amount of compensation recoverable by a victim of discrimination.

28. In its second question, the House of Lords asks whether Article 6 requires (a) that the compensation for the damage sustained as a result of the illegal discrimination should be full and (b) that it should include an award of interest on the principal amount from the date of the unlawful discrimination to the date when compensation is paid.

29. The Court' s interpretation of Article 6 as set out above provides a direct reply to the first part of the second question relating to the level of compensation required by that provision.

30. It also follows from that interpretation that the fixing of an upper limit of the kind at issue in the main proceedings cannot, by definition, constitute proper implementation of Article 6 of the Directive, since it limits the amount of compensation a priori to a level which is not necessarily consistent with the requirement of ensuring real equality of opportunity through adequate reparation for the loss and damage sustained as a result of discriminatory dismissal.

31. With regard to the second part of the second question relating to the award of interest, suffice it to say that full compensation for the loss and damage sustained as a result of discriminatory dismissal cannot leave out of account factors, such as the effluxion of time, which may in fact reduce its value. The award of interest, in accordance with the applicable national rules, must therefore be regarded as an essential component of compensation for the purposes of restoring real equality of treatment.

32. Accordingly, the reply to be given to the first and second questions is that the interpretation of Article 6 of the Directive must be that reparation of the loss and damage sustained by a person injured as a result of discriminatory dismissal may not be limited to an upper limit fixed a priori or by excluding an award of interest to compensate for the loss sustained by the recipient of the compensation as a result of the effluxion of time until the capital sum awarded is actually paid.

THE THIRD QUESTION

33. In its third question, the House of Lords seeks to establish whether a person who has been injured as a result of discriminatory dismissal may rely, as against an authority of the State acting in its capacity as employer, on Article 6 of the Directive in order to contest the application of national rules which impose limits on the amount of compensation recoverable by way of reparation.

34. It follows from the considerations set out above as to the meaning and scope of Article 6 of the Directive, that that provision is an essential factor for attaining the fundamental objective of equal treatment for men and women, in particular as regards working conditions, including the conditions governing dismissal, referred to in Article 5(1) of the Directive, and that, where, in the event of discriminatory dismissal, financial compensation is the measure adopted in order to restore that equality, such compensa-

tion must be full and may not be limited a priori in terms of its amount.

35. Accordingly, the combined provisions of Article 6 and Article 5 of the Directive give rise, on the part of a person who has been injured as a result of discriminatory dismissal, to rights which that person must be able to rely upon before the national courts as against the State and authorities which are an emanation of the State.

NILS DRAEHMPAEHL v URANIA IMMOBILIENSERVICE OHG

[1997] ECR I–02195 (E.C.J.)

2. Those questions [referred by the German Labour Court] were raised in proceedings between Nils Draehmpaehl and Urania Immobilienservice ohG (hereinafter 'Urania') for reparation of damage allegedly suffered by Mr. Draehmpaehl as a result of discrimination on grounds of sex in the making of an appointment.

* * *

7. The relevant provisions of national law concerning equal treatment of men and women in matters of employment are contained in the Bürgerliches Gesetzbuch (German Civil Code, hereinafter 'the BGB').

* * *

9. Paragraph 611a(2) of the BGB provides that if, in the establishment of an employment relationship, an employer becomes liable for a breach of the prohibition of discrimination laid down in subparagraph (1), the applicant discriminated against may claim appropriate financial compensation not exceeding three months' earnings. A month's earnings is to be what the applicant would have been entitled to earn, in cash and in kind, by working normal hours in the month in which an employment relationship should have been established.

11. Paragraph 61b(2) of the Arbeitsgerichtsgesetz (Law on the Organization of Labour Courts, hereinafter 'the ArbGG') provides that, if a number of persons who have been discriminated against in the establishment of an employment relationship claim in legal proceedings compensation pursuant to Paragraph 611a(2) of the BGB, the aggregate amount of the awards of compensation is to be limited, upon application by the employer, to six months' earnings or, when a single recruitment procedure was carried out by the employer with the aim of establishing several employment relationships, to 12 months' earnings. Where the employer has already satisfied claims for compensation, the maximum amount, as

laid down in the first sentence, is to be reduced proportionately. If the compensation to which the plaintiffs would be entitled exceeds in total that maximum amount, the individual awards of compensation are to be reduced in the proportion which their aggregate bears to that maximum amount.

Mr. Draehmpaehl applied by letter dated 17 November 1994 for a post advertised by Urania in the daily newspaper Hamburger Abendblatt. The advertisement was worded as follows:

> "We are seeking an experienced female assistant in our sales management department. If you can get along with the chaotic members of a sales-orientated firm, are willing to make them coffee, get little praise and can work hard, you are the right person for us. We need someone who is able to work on the computer and think with and for others. If you can really face this challenge, we await your application with documents giving full information. But do not say we have not warned you . . .".

Urania did not reply to Mr. Draehmpaehl's letter, nor did it return the documents accompanying his application.

13. Claiming that he was the best qualified applicant for the position and that he had suffered discrimination on grounds of sex in the making of an appointment, Mr. Draehmpaehl brought proceedings in the Arbeitsgericht Hamburg for reparation of damage by payment of compensation equal to three-and-a-half months' earnings.

14. [A]nother male candidate has also brought proceedings for compensation against Urania on similar grounds.

15. The Arbeitsgericht took the view that the plaintiff had been discriminated against by Urania on the grounds of his sex since its job advertisement was formulated in terms which were not neutral and was clearly addressed to women. It also found that there were no clear grounds which would justify an exception, and concluded that Urania was in principle bound to pay compensation to the plaintiff. However, it also took the view that the outcome of the proceedings depended on interpretation of Community law. It therefore decided to stay proceedings and to refer questions to the Court for a preliminary ruling[.]

* * *

23. By [the second and third questions], which should be examined together, the Arbeitsgericht asks in substance whether the Directive precludes provisions of domestic law which place a ceiling of three months' salary on the amount of compensation which may be claimed by applicants discriminated against on grounds of their sex in the making of appointments. It also asks

whether the answer to that question applies equally to applicants who were discriminated against in the recruitment procedure but who, owing to the superior qualifications of the applicant engaged, would not have obtained the position even if the selection process had been free of discrimination and to those who were discriminated against in the recruitment procedure and who would have obtained the position to be filled if selection had been carried out without discrimination.

24. In this regard, it must be pointed out first of all that, even though the Directive does not impose a specific sanction on the Member States, nevertheless Article 6 obliges them to adopt measures which are sufficiently effective for achieving the aim of the Directive and to ensure that those measures may be effectively relied on before the national courts by the persons concerned (Case 14/83 Von Colson and Kamann v. Land Nordrhein–Westfalen [1984] ECR 1891, paragraph 18).

25. Moreover, the Directive requires that, if a Member State chooses to penalize breach of the prohibition of discrimination by the award of compensation, that compensation must be such as to guarantee real and effective judicial protection, have a real deterrent effect on the employer and must in any event be adequate in relation to the damage sustained. Purely nominal compensation would not satisfy the requirements of an effective transposition of the Directive (*Von Colson and Kamann*, paragraphs 23 and 24).

26. Similarly, the German Government's argument that compensation consisting of a maximum of three months' salary is more than nominal and represents an appreciable, considerable and dissuasive financial burden, thus awarding the person discriminated against appreciable compensation, cannot be regarded as well founded.

27. As the Court held in paragraph 23 of its judgment in *Von Colson and Kamann*, once the Member States choose to make good damage suffered as a result of discrimination prohibited by the Directive pursuant to rules governing employers' civil liability, the compensation awarded must be adequate in relation to the damage sustained.

28. Moreover, it is clear from the order for reference, from the answers given to the questions put by the Court and from the explanations given at the hearing that the provisions of German law applicable in the case before the national court place on compensation a specific ceiling which is not provided for by other provisions of domestic civil and labour law.

29. In choosing the appropriate solution for guaranteeing that the objective of the Directive is attained, the Member States must ensure that infringements of Community law are penalized under

conditions, both procedural and substantive, which are analogous to those applicable to infringements of domestic law of a similar nature and importance (Case 68/88 Commission v. Greece [1989] ECR 2965, paragraph 24).

30. It follows from the foregoing that provisions of domestic law which, unlike other provisions of domestic civil law and labour law, prescribe an upper limit of three months' salary for the compensation which may be obtained in the event of discrimination on grounds of sex in the making of an appointment do not fulfil those requirements.

31. The question which must therefore be considered is whether that answer applies equally to job applicants who, because the successful applicant had superior qualifications, would not have obtained the position, even if the selection process had been free of discrimination, and to those who would have obtained the position if selection process had been carried out without discrimination.

32. In this regard, it must be borne in mind that, as paragraphs 25 and 27 of this judgment make clear, reparation must be adequate in relation to the damage sustained.

33. Nevertheless, such reparation may take account of the fact that, even if there had been no discrimination in the selection process, some applicants would not have obtained the position to be filled since the applicant appointed had superior qualifications. It is indisputable that such applicants, not having suffered any damage through exclusion from the recruitment procedure, cannot claim that the extent of the damage they have sustained is the same as that sustained by applicants who would have obtained the position if there had been no discrimination in the selection process.

34. Consequently, the only damage suffered by an applicant belonging to the first category mentioned in paragraph 31 above is that resulting from the failure, as a result of discrimination on grounds of sex, to take his application into consideration, whereas an applicant belonging to the second category has suffered damage as a result of a refusal to engage him, owing, specifically, to the objectively erroneous assessment of his application, as a result of discrimination on grounds of sex, made by the employer.

35. Having regard to those considerations, it does not seem unreasonable for a Member State to lay down a statutory presumption that the damage suffered by an applicant belonging to the first category may not exceed a ceiling of three months' salary.

36. In this regard, it must be made clear it is for the employer, who has in his possession all the applications submitted, to

adduce proof that the applicant would not have obtained the vacant position even if there had been no discrimination.

* * *

38. By its fourth question the Arbeitsgericht asks in substance whether the Directive precludes provisions of domestic law imposing a ceiling on the aggregate amount of compensation payable to several applicants discriminated against on the grounds of their sex in the making of an appointment.

* * *

40. It is clear that a provision such as Paragraph 61b(2) of the ArbGG, which places a ceiling of six months' salary on the aggregate amount of compensation for all applicants harmed by discrimination on grounds of sex in the making of an appointment, where several applicants claim compensation, may lead to the award of reduced compensation and may have the effect of dissuading applicants so harmed from asserting their rights. Such a consequence would not represent real and effective judicial protection and would have no really dissuasive effect on the employer, as required by the Directive.

41. Moreover, it is clear from the order for reference, from the answers to the questions put by the Court and from the explanations given at the hearing that such a ceiling on the aggregate compensation is not prescribed by other provisions of domestic civil law or labour law.

42. However, as the Court has already held, the procedures and conditions governing a right to reparation based on Community law must not be less favourable than those laid down by comparable national rules (Case 68/88 Commission v. Greece, paragraph 24).

43. The answer to the question must therefore be that the Directive precludes provisions of domestic law which, unlike other provisions of domestic civil and labour law, impose a ceiling of six months' salary on the aggregate amount of compensation which, where several applicants claim compensation, may be claimed by applicants who have been discriminated against on grounds of their sex in the making of an appointment.

SCHULER-ZGRAGGEN v SWITZERLAND

(1996) 21 E.H.R.R. 404 (E.C.H.R.)

2. In a judgment of 24 June 1993 ("the principal judgment") the Court found that there had been a breach of Article 14 of the Convention taken together with Article 6(1), as the assumption

that women gave up work when they gave birth to a child had been the sole basis for the reasoning in a judgment of the Federal Insurance Court and had introduced a difference of treatment on the ground of sex only, a difference that lacked any reasonable and objective justification.

The Court ruled that its judgment constituted in itself sufficient just satisfaction in respect of the alleged non-pecuniary damage and that the respondent State was to pay the applicant, within three months, 7,500 Sfr. in respect of costs and expenses.

3. As the question of the application of Article 50 was not ready for decision as regards the pecuniary damage, it was reserved in the principal judgment.

4. On 7 April 1994 the Agent of the Government informed the President that in a judgment of 24 March 1994 the Federal Insurance Court had concluded the rehearing proceedings commenced under section 139a of the Federal Judicature Act. Its own judgment of 21 June 1988 had been set aside, and the applicant had been granted a full invalidity pension with effect from 1 May 1986.

5. On 27 April 1994 Counsel for the applicant advised the Registrar that his client did not consider that the proceedings in Switzerland were terminated and that she had submitted to the Department of Finance a claim for compensation in the amount of 40,933.64 Sfr. based on section 3 of the Act on the liability of the Confederation.

7. On 14 September 1994 the applicant's representative sent the Registrar a copy of the Federal Council's decision of 12 June 1994 whereby the compensation claim was refused; he asked the Court to consider the possibility of ruling on his client's claims as an agreement with the Government seemed unlikely.

10. Under Article 50 of the Convention,

> If the Court finds that a decision or a measure taken by a legal authority or any other authority of a High Contracting Party is completely or partially in conflict with the obligations arising from the ... Convention, and if the internal law of the said Party allows only partial reparation to be made for the consequences of this decision or measure, the decision of the Court shall, if necessary, afford just satisfaction to the injured party.

14. The Court takes note of the rehearing proceedings under section 139a of the Federal Judicature Act which, following its principal judgment, took place in the Federal Insurance Court and culminated in the applicant's being awarded a full invalidity pension with effect from 1 May 1986. It fully appreciates the importance of that court's judgment of 24 March 1994 for the execution

of judgments delivered at Strasbourg; the Federal Insurance Court thereby showed its commitment to the Convention and the Court's case law.

15. The only issue remaining to be determined is that of the interest claimed by Mrs. Schuler–Zgraggen on the invalidity pension received between 1 May 1986 and 20 April 1994.

The Court reiterates that "just satisfaction" is to be afforded "if necessary" and that it is not bound in the matter by any national legal rule in this instance the Federal Insurance Court's case law on the awarding of interest. It consequently considers that it is not for the European Court to pass judgment on the merits in Swiss law of the Federal Insurance Court's decision in which the claim in issue was disallowed. It suffices for it to note that, at the end of fresh proceedings following the Strasbourg judgment, the Federal Insurance Court recognised that the applicant was entitled to a full pension and gave retrospective effect to that recognition. In so doing, it intended to make reparation for the damage resulting from the breach of the Convention. However, it did not take into account the passing of time—about eight years. It therefore appears justified under the Convention to award some interest for the period in question.

Note: Equal Treatment Directive 2002/73

The European Union imposes enforcement responsibilities on each member country. Thus, under Article 6(2) of the Equal Treatment Directive [2002/73],

> Member States shall introduce into their national legal systems such measures as are necessary to ensure real and effective compensation or reparation as the Member States so determine for the loss and damage sustained by a person injured as a result of discrimination contrary to Article 3, in a way which is dissuasive and proportionate to the damage suffered; such compensation or reparation may not be restricted by the fixing of a prior upper limit, except in cases where the employer can prove that the only damage suffered by an applicant as a result of discrimination within the meaning of this Directive is the refusal to take his/her job application into consideration.

In addition, Article 8 now provides:

> Member States shall lay down the rules on sanctions applicable to infringements of the national provisions adopted pursuant to this Directive, and shall take all measures necessary to ensure that they are applied. The sanctions, which may comprise the payment of compensation to the victim, must be effective, proportionate and dissuasive.

Article 8 also requires member states to maintain enforcement agencies. Article 6(3) provides:

> Member States shall ensure that associations, organisations or other legal entities which have, in accordance with the criteria laid down by their national law, a legitimate interest in ensuring that the provisions of this Directive are complied with, may engage, either on behalf or in support of the complainants, with his or her approval, in any judicial and/or administrative procedure provided for the enforcement of obligations under this Directive.

Notes and Questions

1. **Effectiveness of Lost-Pay Remedy?** Do new Articles 6(2) and 8 change the law reflected in the cases above? Is payment of lost wages to an individual "effective, proportionate and dissuasive" in a case involving systemic discrimination? In a case of sexual harassment, where the victim continued to draw a salary? Do these articles suggest that systemic change through injunctive relief might sometimes be required?

2. **Remedies for Failure of Member States to Enforce EU Directives?** Will Article 6(3) allow suits that are basically class actions, even though national law does not allow class actions against employment discrimination? What remedies are available to individuals whose nations fail to follow EU law? May they bring suit to enforce EU law? Note that Article 226 of the EU Treaty provides:

> If the Commission considers that a Member State has failed to fulfil an obligation under this Treaty, it shall deliver a reasoned opinion on the matter after giving the State concerned the opportunity to submit its observations.
>
> If the State concerned does not comply with the opinion within the period laid down by the Commission, the latter may bring the matter before the Court of Justice.

B. ENFORCEMENT MECHANISMS

SAMUEL ESTREICHER, UNJUST DISMISSAL LAWS: SOME CAUTIONARY NOTES

33 Am. J. Comp. L. 310 (1985)

I. American. Exceptionalism

We have always felt a measure of pride in American exceptionalism. By and large, the issue of race apart, our society has been largely free of the rigid class barriers and pervasive class consciousness that mar the industrial history and continue to rend the social fabric of many of the European countries I will be discussing, Some explanation can be found in Frederick Turner's "open frontier", the opportunities afforded by our ever-expanding frontier (often working considerable in-justice to "Native Americans"). Immigration, providing a continuous supply of unskilled laborers who saw America as a land of opportunity-whatever the reality-also provides a key. In sum, our relatively open society, or at least the widespread perception of openness, has acted as a continuing corrosive on class divisions (in the European sense of the term).

* * *

Increasingly, however, our exceptionalism has come to be viewed in negative terms. We seem to stand virtually alone among the nations of the Western industrialized world in not providing general protection against unjust discharge for private-sector employees who either cannot or do not choose unionism. We also appear to be unique in failing at the government level to provide meaningful protection for employees displaced by economic dismissals and plant terminations. Comparative labor law permits us to reexamine deeply embedded assumptions about our own employment law system. If we are indeed "backward" in these areas as some have claimed, we must ask why? As Mark Twain put it, "Few things are harder to put up with than the annoyance of a good example." The question is: should we be "annoyed"?

II. Overview of Other Countries

I think it useful to begin with a rather straightforward account of the unjust dismissal statutes in Canada and some of the Western European countries.

A. Canada

With the legal culture and collective bargaining system most like our own, Canada would seem the most promising example for our purposes.

In Canada, labor legislation operates on two levels: federal and provincial.

1. Federal Legislation

In 1978, the Canadian Labour Code was amended to protect against unjust dismissal employees who have been with the same employer for at least twelve months and are not subject to a collective agreement.[5] This measure applies only to industries within the federal sector—largely, the transportation, communications and atomic energy fields-comprising a thin layer, about 1/10th of

5. Canada Labour Code § 61.5; see Statutes of Canada, 1977–1978, 26–27 Eliz. II * * *. [Eds. The provision is now at § 240 of the Code; the applicable procedure is at §§ 241–46.]

the non-agricultural workforce (which, in turn, is no more than 1/10th of our own labor force).

A discharged employee may bring his complaint to a government inspector who will attempt conciliation. If that fails, the employee can petition the Minister of Labour, who, in his discretion, may appoint an adjudicator to hear the complaint. The adjudicator's decision is final, binding and unreviewable in any court. These adjudicators, drawn largely from the ranks of private labor arbitrators, apply conventional labor arbitration principles and are authorized to award reinstatement with back pay. Reinstatement, though discretionary, appears to be routinely awarded * * * ; no statistics are presently available, however, on the survival rate of reinstatees. Canadian labor law specialists tell me that managerial employees have with increasing success also pursued their common law right to dismissal only upon notice, absent "just cause". In some cases, mid-level managers have secured judgments providing for 3 years' salary in lieu of notice.

2. *Provincial Laws*

Given the limits of federal legislative authority, however, labor law in Canada is largely a provincial matter. Most of the Provinces require that, absent "just cause", significant periods of notice (depending upon years of service) precede discharge. In many, awards of one year's pay in lieu of notice for mid-level managers are not uncommon. Some of the provincial statutes, however, stipulate precise, shorter notice periods (often keyed to regular pay intervals). In 1975, Nova Scotia enacted legislation providing "just cause" protection for dismissal—even with notice-for employees with 10 years of service with the same employer; and in 1980, Quebec passed unjust dismissal legislation for employees with at least five years of service.[7]

B. *Great Britain*

Since 1971, Parliament has provided general statutory protection against unjust dismissal. The law, which has undergone several revisions, includes professionals and managers, but excludes (i) employees with less than 52 continuous weeks of service (a two-year qualifying period applies, moreover, in the case of discharges from firms having twenty or fewer employees); (ii) men over 65 years of age and women over 60; and (iii) employees under a fixed term contract of at least one year's duration who have waived in

7. Nova Scotia Labour Standards Code 67(A)(1) * * *; S.Q. 179, c. 45, as amended, s.124 * * *. [Eds. The proposition that reasonable notice of termination is required absent "just cause" would seem not to be firmly established across Canada. See Wallace v. United Grain Growers Ltd., [1997] 3 S.C.R. 701, [1997] S.C.J. No. 94 (Supreme Court of Canada, 1997).]

writing any statutory claims (apparently, such waivers can be secured at the outset of the employment relationship).[8]

The burden is on the employer to show a legitimate reason for the discharge such as lack of competence, misconduct or "some other substantial reason of a kind to justify" dismissal (the latter, a catch-all phrase that in practice gives employers a great deal of leeway). If the employer clears this hurdle, the tribunal must then decide—without allocating the burden of persuasion to either side—whether the dismissal was fair, taking into account all of the circumstances "including the size and administrative resources of the employer's undertaking".[9] Studies show that a great deal of deference is paid to managerial prerogative, with little substantive review of reasons given. Moreover, the law has been interpreted to require only good faith and reasonable belief, not that the employee in fact has committed the infraction.[11] Also, procedural irregularities are otherwise condoned where such justification is in any event present.[12]

Complaints are initially referred to the Advisory, Conciliation and Arbitration Service (ACAS) for attempted conciliation, Most complaints are resolved at this stage. If unsuccessful, the complaint goes to a tripartite industrial tribunal for hearing. The tribunal is not bound by strict rules of evidence, and counsel in theory are not necessary but increasingly resorted to. Appeals lie to an Employment Appeals Tribunal (EAT), and to the general courts on questions of law.

Reinstatement is authorized but discretionary; the tribunal is instructed by statute to consider the employee's wishes, the practicability of reinstatement, and any employee fault. Presently, a majority of complainants apparently prefer compensation, though it has been argued that this preference stems from misinformation about their rights and a sense that reinstatement will ultimately

8. [Eds. Current provisions are in Parts IX–X of the Employment Protection (Consolidation) Act of 1996. The right not to be unfairly dismissed does not apply (1) unless the employee "has been continuously employed for a period of not less than two years ending with the effective date of termination" id. § 108; (2) the employee has reached "normal retiring age for an employee holding [that] position" or age of 65, id. § 109. As a result of 1999 legislation, it is not longer possible for an employer and employee to enter into a legally enforceable fixed-term agreement that purports to exclude nonrenewal of such an agreement from unjust dismissal protections. See also Fixed–Term Employees (Prevention of Less Favourable Treatment) Regulations 2002, S.I. 2002/2034.]

9. [Eds. § 98(4) of the Employment Protection (Consolidation) Act of 1996.]

11. See Bob Hepple, 5 Intl. Encyc. Labour Law and Indus. Rel. ¶ 285, at 189 (R. Blanpain ed., 1980).

12. See Bob Hepple, The British Experience with Unfair Dismissals Legislation, in Arbitration Issues of the 1980s: Proc. of the 34th Ann. Mgt. of the Natl. Academy of Arbitrators 24 (Stern & Dennis eds., 1981).

result in another dismissal.[13]

Even where employees plainly wish to be reinstated or reengaged (reemployed elsewhere in the same firm), by all accounts the tribunals are most reluctant, deferring virtually to a man to the employer's wishes. Despite statutory amendment to make explicit a preference for reinstatement where practicable, the trend is to avoid this remedy altogether. Bob Hepple, chairman of Industrial Tribunals in England and Wales, reports that in 1973, 4.2% of those whose cases were settled prior to hearing were given back their jobs; this figure dropped to 1.8% in 1979. Similarly, in 1973, 2.3% of those going to hearing got their jobs back; by 1979, this figure plummeted to 0.8%. Even where reinstatement is ordered, employers can pay an additional award in lieu of reinstatement. And where employers comply with reinstatement orders, only 80% of the employees return and many do not stay long on the job. Moreover, the statute does not at present monitor ongoing post-award compliance.

Thus, the principal British remedy is a monetary award, typically in three segments: (i) a basic award calculated, like a redundancy payment, in terms of age and years of service, subject as of 1982 to a maximum £3,600; (ii) a compensatory award, subject to deductions for mitigated earnings and other payment from the employer (including unemployment insurance); and (iii) where compliance with a reinstatement order is not forthcoming, an additional award (of between 13–26 weeks wages). Actual awards are quite modest. In 1978, despite a potential maximum of £13,400, the median award was £375 (about 5 weeks' net pay at the average wage); and 3/4 of the awards were for less than £750.[17]

C. *Germany*

A 1951 statute proscribes "socially unwarranted" dismissals defined as dismissals "not based on reasons connected with the person or [his conduct] . . . or [not based] on urgent social needs that preclude his continued employment. . . ." In theory, notice must precede most discharges, and dismissals without cause of

13. See Williams & Lewis, Legislating for Job Security: The British Experience of Reinstatement and Reengagement, 8 Employee Rels. L. J. 482 (Winter 1982–83).

17. [Eds. "The maximum award for compensation [was] limited to £56,800 from 1 February 2005 and £58,400 from 1 February 2006. Awards may be above the maximum where they include a basic award element." Employment Tribunal Service, Annual Report & Accounts 1005–06, App., table 4, at 30. In 2005–06, the median unfair-dismissal award issued by the employment tribunals was £4,228 and the average award was £8,679. A little under 6% of the awards were over £30,000. Ibid. In discrimination cases, where the amount of damages is potentially unlimited, the median race discrimination award was £6,640, the median sex discrimination award was £5,546, and the median disability discrimination award was £9,021; the average awards in these categories were, respectively, £30,361, £10,807, and £19,-360. Id., tables 5–7, at 31.]

employees with at least six months' employment with firms having more than five employees are legally ineffective to dissolve the employment relationship.

The German scheme is very closely tied to the works council institution. Under 1972 legislation, the works council—which is quite widespread though not universally established among all firms with five or more employee—is elected by all employees on the shop floor, and is empowered to vote on (and often does veto) many important decisions governing the workplace, e.g., new overtime, piece-work policies. The law requires that employers given advance notice of all dismissals to the council, where one exists. Should the council object, employers are likely, especially in the larger firms, to back down, rather than antagonize a group whose cooperation is essential on other matters. If employers, however, persist with the dismissal—usually in the case of an alleged grave offense, such as an assault or a wildcat strike—the works council's objection has the legal effect of forcing retention of the employee pendente life.[19] Such provisional retention, however, occurs quite rarely. The works council must give detailed reasons in a very formal manner if it intends to interpose an objection. Moreover, the employer can attempt to convince the tripartite Labor Court that keeping the employee on the job would be unjust or pose an intolerable economic burden. Reinstatement is rarely awarded once the Labor Court has sanctioned a severance of the relationship; in such cases, the employee settles for damages and does not wait for the results of what will often be a prolonged litigation. Indeed, mitigation and unemployment insurance policies virtually compel the employee promptly to seek employment elsewhere. Even if the court finds that a dismissal has been unjustified, the employer can avoid reinstatement by paying up to twelve to eighteen months' salary if there is reason to believe that any further cooperation between the employer and the employee is unlikely to serve the purposes of the firm. As one observer has noted, "the protection against dismissal does not really preserve the job but gives only a right to compensation."[24]

D. *France*

In 1973, France went beyond its "abus de droit", or abuse of right, doctrine to provide employees with a right to a pre-dismissal

19. The Works Constitution Act of 1972 § 102(5).

24. Ramm, Federal Republic of Germany, 5 Intl. Encyc. Labour Law and Indus. Rel. ¶ 402, at 138 (R. Blanpain, ed. 1979). "In about 2–5 percent of all protection against dismissal suits the employee is kept in his employment." Id. ¶ 393, at 136. [Eds. For an update, see Manfred Weiss & Marlene Schmidt, Federal Republic of Germany, 6 Intl. Encyc. Labour Law and Indus. Rel. ¶¶ 235–242, at 108–113 (R. Blanpain, ed.) (updated to March 1, 2000). Professors Weiss and Schmidt report that decisions of the Federal Labour Court in 1985 strengthened the reinstatement remedy. See ¶ 240, at 111.]

hearing and to extend protection against discharge without "serious and genuine cause" to all employees with at least two years' service at firms having at least eleven employees. Reinstatement may be proposed but (except for discharge of worker representatives) compliance is entirely optional and rare. If there is no reinstatement, an employer must pay at least six months' compensation in addition to statutorily mandated severance pay (though unlike Great Britain, without deduction for mitigated earnings). The awards rendered in lieu of restatement rarely exceed the minimum six-month period. Adjudication occurs in special labor courts with non-career judges elected by employers and employees nationwide; professional judges are called in only in cases of deadlock and presided over by a professional judge. Quite aside from formal burdens of proof, the court plays an inquisitorial role. To avoid liability, employers often clothe discharge in economic terms to come within less onerous redundancy dismissal rules.

Legislation enacted by the Mitterand Government in 1982 prohibits dismissal of employees because of political or religious convictions; and requires employers to develop internal rules governing dismissal and to consult with newly established enterprise committees (mandatory for all firms with at least fifty employees) or employee delegates prior to effecting the dismissal.[27]

E. Italy

All terminated employees are entitled to severance pay and advance notice of termination. Moreover, all employees in firms with more than fifteen workers, if not under collective agreements, are statutorily protected against unjust discharge. Should a court proceeding, in which the employer has the burden of persuasion, result in a finding of unjustified dismissal, an employee can obtain reinstatement and an indemnity award (which at a minimum must equal five months' salary). Reinstatement appears to be more frequent here than elsewhere on the Continent.) Under a separate procedure, executive employees can sue for up to twenty months' indemnity, but cannot obtain reinstatement.[31]

27. See Michel Despax 7 Jacques Rojot, France, in 5 Intl. Encyc. Labour Law and Indus. Rel. ¶¶ 236–39, at 103–04 (R. Blanpain, ed. 1979).; Rojot, Protections Against Unfair Dismissal in France, app. B, in Stieber & Blackburn, Protecting Unorganized Employees Against Unjust Discharge 147(Michigan State Univ., 1983).

31. [Eds. "If the dismissal was held to lack just cause [under Act No. 604] * * * [the employer] was bound to reinstate the worker within three days, or, alternatively, to pay a special indemnity assessed on the same basis as the 1965 agreement. This solution, which does not in fact guarantee reinstatement of the discharged employee, has been radically changed by Article 18 of Act No. 300 of 1970 and lately by Act 108/1990. Article 18 empowers the judge (pretoire) to order reinstatement in any case of unjustified, discriminatory or formally vitiated dismissal. * * * [Act 108] furthermore gives to employees unjustly discharge the right to ask for monetary compensation for up to 15 months of

F. Japan

Japan's labor relations system, so much a part of what appears to be a vastly different social, economic and political culture, at first glance does not belong in this survey. However, in many ways, post World War II labor law in Japan began with the American model, and thus the Japanese experience should teach us something about the role of socio-cultural variables. Whatever the analytical reason, Japan's success as our major importer and competitor in so many areas compels inclusion.

* * *

Statutory law goes no further than thirty days' advance notice or pay (in lieu of notice), absent just cause. A number of commentators, however, have identified the emergence of general "just cause" protection for all employees, presumably flowing from academic and judicial elaboration of the "good faith" principle found in article 27 of the Constitution and the "abuse of right" principle in Article 1(3) of the Civil Code.[34] Certainly, where the policy of shusin koyo, or permanent employment, is practiced, principally in the larger firms—comprising about a third of the nonagricultural workforce—employers are reluctant to discharge their so-called "regular" workers; and just cause may indeed be implicit in the representations made to those employees.

The underlying reality, however, may not be one of significant job security. In many ways, the shusin koyo sector is run on the same principles as a Wall Street-type law firm: at some point in the process you learn that you are not on the "sure track" to partnership, and while not dismissed, you are expected with subtle pressure mounting each year-and out of pride, if nothing more, to find another niche for yourself in the world; and in time, you do. Early retirement in Japan, secured by financial blandishments (taishokin) and other pressures, such as the "tap on the shoulder" system of katatatake, is also an important feature of the system. As one observer has remarked, "the Japanese have lifetime employment among the young, and the Americans have it among the old." [36]

salary in lieu of reinstatement." T. Treu, Italy, in 6 Intl. Encyc. Labour Law and Indus. Rel. ¶ ¶ 15–220, 109–111 (R. Blanpain, ed.) (monograph updated to January 2006).]

34. [Eds. See Tadashi A. Hanami & Fumito Komiya, Japan, in 6 Intl. Encyc. Labour Law and Indus. Rel. ¶ 195, 124–25 (R. Blanpain, ed.) (monograph updated to November 2005). In 2003, the judicial developments were codified in Article 18(2) of the Labour Standards Law, quoted in id. at 125: "if dismissal is found to be without any rational reason and not to be permissible with regard to the common sense of society, such dismissal is void because of abuse of the employer's right of dismissal."]

36. Solomon B. Levine, Japanese Industrial Relations: What Can We Import?, 26th NYU Annual Conf. on Labor § 2.03[1], at 2–11 (1983) * * *.

One mistake many Americans make about Japan is to assume that the shushin kayo sector is representative of the entire workforce. Life-time employment is confined to large-scale firms (typically with 500 or more employees), comprising no more than one-third of the nonagricultural workforce. The overwhelming majority of Japanese workers are engaged by small enterprises or are self-employed. Moreover, few private firms admit women to regular, long-term status, thus excluding from eligibility for shushin koyo about one-third of the entire labor force. As Professor Roberts has noted, Japan has a pervasive dual labor market, with a secondary sector of temporary workers and employees of subcontractors providing "elements of labor cost flexibility." [38]

When we depart from shushin koyo and turn to the temporary employees and subcontractors that serve as "shock absorbers" for the major firms—providing labor and subsidiary services when needed, withdrawing from the picture when not—it is a little difficult to understand the assertion of general "just cause" protection. For employees in the secondary sector, in comparison with their counterparts in the primary sector, Professor Roberts tells us, the situation is one of "less employment security, higher levels of labor turnover, less optimum health and safety conditions, weaker employees' unions, and more aristocratic management." Apparently, some judicial decisions have found a "good faith" limitation on the ability of the major firms to refuse to re-engage temporary workers whose fixed-term contracts had been previously renewed-a kind of "chain" theory of job security. This may be a harbinger of things to come.

Mention should also be made of the provisional injunction practice that may serve to help employees remain on the job pendente life, and thereby raise the cost of disagreement for the employer. I suspect, however, that such employees feel considerable pressure to effect a prompt lateral transfer even when they get an injunction.

III. General, Characteristics of Unjust Dismissal Laws Abroad

4. Reinstatement

The most striking point about the foregoing. schemes is that, irrespective of formal legal position, reinstatement is simply not an important feature in practice (at least outside of Canada, Italy and perhaps Germany). The measures surveyed here do not in fact vindicate a right to a job. At best, they provide a much needed transfer payment to cushion displacement and perhaps an opportunity to clear one's name.

38. Roberts, Issues in British and Japanese Industrial Relations Systems, 2 J. Japanese Trade & Industry 20, 21 (1984).

The evidence from England and from studies of NLRB reinstatees, as compared with labor arbitration reinstatees, suggests that the rein-statement remedy is difficult to police effectively outside of the context of union representation. Germany's works councils seem to play a supportive role, similar to that of a union, and Italy's statute is aided by its labor movement's willingness to assist nonmember dischargees (in the hopes of recruiting them). One may venture here the generalization that perhaps such protective support mechanisms are necessary to the success of the reinstatement remedy.

5. Size of Awards

Outside of Canada and possibly Italy, the monetary awards, while not insignificant, are at modest, predictable levels—certainly in comparison to American jury recoveries. The English awards are striking in this regard, which goes a long way toward explaining the English employers' reluctance to reinstate and the high settlement rate prior to hearing. Punitive damages are also not a significant feature, although punitive concepts explain the additional award in Great Britain's statute and other similar provisions.

C. Exclusions from Coverage and Fixed–Term Contracts

None of the countries in question provide universal protection; throughout we find qualifying periods of continuous service * * * [and limitations by size of employers subject to the law.]

Managerial employees apparently are not per se excluded from coverage. (Italy does provide a separate set of procedures.) Great Britain's exclusion of employees under fixed-term contract of at least one year's duration may operate to disqualify most managers, Even if formally excluded, however, managerial employees may have common law rights to dismissal only upon notice.

As to fixed-term contracts, Great Britain permits exclusion in the case of employees under a fixed-term contract of at least one year's du-ration who sign a written waiver of statutory rights. On the other hand, Germany, France and Italy, sensing here a potentially significant evasive tactic, seek to discourage repeated renewal of fixed term contracts.

D. Delegation of "Just Cause" Criteria to the Tribunal

None of the statutes here attempt to spell out the standards, the criteria of "just cause." Rather, they are broad delegations to the tribunals to develop procedural and substantive criteria, usually without guidance from a well-developed body of labor arbitration law.

The British model, as it has evolved, seems to be one of deferential review of managerial prerogative, rather than de nova review similar in theory to our judicial review of administrative agency action. This model of thoroughgoing deference seems not to have taken hold else-where on the Continent.

E. Use of Specialized Tribunals

With the exception of Japan and Italy, the statutes in question all utilize specialized labor tribunals that, at least in theory, are thought to dispense a cheaper, quicker, more accessible and expert justice. These tribunals, while often tripartite, do not offer the same opportunity for party selection of decisionmaker as would U.S. labor arbitration.

F. Absence of Labor Union Opposition

Although at first unions were skeptical, even opposed, to these new statutes, the evidence strongly suggests that the European unions have not only made their peace but also have assisted nonmember utilization of the statutory procedures (as an organizing tactic).

G. Relation to Redundancy Dismissal Legislation

Virtually all of the countries under review have also enacted some protections against economic dismissals, individual or group. In Great Britain, redundancy laws preceded the unjust dismissal statute. Although I am not sure of the precise relationship between these schemes, I, suspect that unjust dismissal laws appeared to many as at least logically inevitable once the inviolability of the at-will concept was breached by redundancy laws. Moreover, in many situations, both disciplinary and economic reasons may be potentially available to an employer bent on terminating an employee. Effective policing of either scheme may well require enactment of the other.

IV. Some Questions Concerning Transplantability; A Partial Agenda for Future Research

As a good, risk-averse teacher, I have left the most difficult for last, and I have only questions concerning transplantability—an agenda for future research-but no answers.

A. Barriers to Understanding the Foreign Schemes

1. Language

Despite an ever growing comparative labor law literature in English, including Roger Blanpain's invaluable International Encyclopedia for Labor Law and Industrial Relations, we can never truly be certain that we are getting all of the nuances of language quite right. Blanpain gives some telling examples, "Eventually" means "inevitably" to us, but for the French, "eventuellement" means "possibly." Another: "arbitration"—in French "arbitrage"—usually means a binding decision by an impartial umpire, but in Luxembourg it refers to a recommendation by a government conciliator.

2. Cultural and Social Context

The social and cultural barriers are even more formidable. It is difficult to make any sense of positive Japanese law without a deep appreciation of the web of cultural preconceptions and pressures that condition, that frame how the law is in fact experienced in the plant. For example, the dismissed employee's ability to secure interim injunctive relief may be quite illusory if the atmosphere at the plant makes life so intolerable that the employee voluntarily quits. If reported as a voluntary termination, this statistic would be meaningless. German unjust dismissal law may seem quite attractive, but we need to know a great deal more than we presently do, not only about the impact of works councils on economic efficiency, but also about their representative quality, their possible exclusion of disfavored minorities, the safeguards against reliance on supposedly irrelevant personal, political criteria in deciding whether or not to object to a given dismissal.

B. Some Areas for Further Research

* * *

3. Reinstatement Remedies

Although a legal system can certainly take the position that reinstatement should be available if only as a bar-gaining chip for an employee who cannot realistically return to his former job, I think more work has to be done on whether, and under what conditions, an effective reinstatement remedy is possible in a nonunionized environment or one without a support mechanism similar to the German works councils. A meaningful reinstatement remedy would also have to provide for post-award policing.

We also have to think hard about the feasibility of compulsory reinstatement of high-level executives or other employees whose jobs re-quire maintenance of a high degree of employer trust and confidence. The question of "contracting out" or waiver is of great significance here. Does a "no waiver" rule make sense in the context of employees who have a fair measure of individual bargaining power? What if waivers are coupled with a meaningful internal grievance system culminating in impartial arbitration?

4. Punitive, Open-ended Damage Awards vs. Relatively Predictable Awards Based Largely on Principles of Compensation?

We have to ask ourselves whether we wish to emulate the European model of unjust dismissal recovery—that is, relatively predictable awards keyed primarily to principles of compensation up to a maximum limit set at a multiple of regular pay—or rather continue with what appears to be an embryonic American model of open-ended jury recoveries and punitive damages, stressing principles of deterrence. The fairly widespread acceptance by European employers of these "just cause" regimes may well be attributable to their ability readily to insure themselves without excessive costs.

5. *Special Labor Tribunals*

What are the costs and benefits for this country, which already suffers from multi-fora remedies and a highly fragmented law of the employment relation? The Canadian federal government's use of "adjudicators" from the ranks of private labor arbitrators seems an attractive possibility, but there are obvious questions of cost. We should also question whether such adjudicators should be permitted freely to rely on conventional labor arbitration concepts. These are principles developed in a consensual setting as part of an ongoing process of collective bargaining. They apply to disputes typically not involving employees whose jobs involve considerable unsupervised time and the daily exercise of discretion and judgment.

The moral force of the foreign experience is unquestionable, at least from the standpoint of fairness to discharged nonunionized or nonorganizable employees. These are indeed "annoying" examples, but our's should not be an uncritical wholesale adoption of any foreign scheme. We have to think hard about certain features of the foreign schemes; about the suitability of certain of our own rules developed for unionized settings; and about whether our litigious culture and trial and jury institutions are likely to upset the delicate balance between fairness and managerial vigor.

Notes and Questions

1. **Relationship Between Discrimination and Unfair Dismissal Claims**. Because of the availability of unfair dismissal remedies in most of the European countries, there may be less of an incentive to frame one's case as a discrimination case where the gravamen of the claim is a challenge to the fairness of a termination decision. Thus, for example, 31% of cases disposed of in 2005–06 involved discrimination claims. See Employment Tribunal Service, Annual Report & Accounts 2005–06, App., table 2, at 29. In the U.S., by contrast, given the absence of unfair dismissal legislation (outside of Montana), plaintiffs look to the anti-discrimination laws as their principal recourse. Over time, litigants in Europe may be more attracted to pursuing discrimination claims which, under EU law, cannot be subject to a maximum level of recovery.

2. **Relatively Low U.K. Tribunal Awards.** By U.S. standards, U.K. employment tribunal awards would seem low, even in discrimina-

tion cases where caps are no longer imposed on such awards (see note 17 of the excerpt). What factors might explain this? The extent of discrimination in the U.K.? The absence of a civil jury? The legal culture in the U.K. Might this be the model for a desirable trade-off for the U.S.—relatively prompt recovery provided in informal employment tribunals but lower awards?

3. **Special Tribunals**? Why have the Europeans tended to provide for special adminsitrative tribunals or labor courts to handle employment cases, including discrimination claims? Would the U.S. need a similar set of institutions to administrative a general unfair dismissal regime?

Note: U.K. Commission for Equality and Human Rights

Until recently, under U.K. law different agencies had responsibility for enforcing the various bans on discrimination in employment. An Equal Opportunities Commission enforced the law against sex discrimination, the Commission on Racial Equality enforced the law against race discrimination, and the Disability Rights Commission enforced the law against discrimination based on disability. However, the Equality Act 2006 creates a Commission for Equality and Human Rights (CEHR), which will take over the responsibilities of the prior agencies and will also enforce laws against discrimination based on religion or sexual orientation. Adjudication remains, however, the function of the Employment Tribunals.

This Commission's duties extend to all unlawful discrimination, not just employment discrimination. Under section 8(1) of the Act:

> (1) The Commission shall, by exercising the powers conferred by this Part—
>
> > (a) promote understanding of the importance of equality and diversity,
> >
> > (b) encourage good practice in relation to equality and diversity,
> >
> > (c) promote equality of opportunity,
> >
> > (d) promote awareness and understanding of rights under the equality enactments,
> >
> > (e) enforce the equality enactments,
> >
> > (f) work towards the elimination of unlawful discrimination, and
> >
> > (g) work towards the elimination of unlawful harassment.

The CEHR is to monitor progress under the non-discrimination laws, may issue codes of practice, conduct inquiries into possible violations, and, under section 20,

(1) The Commission may investigate whether or not a person—

(a) has committed an unlawful act,

(b) has complied with a requirement imposed by an unlawful act notice under section 21, or

(c) has complied with an undertaking given under section 23.

(2) The Commission may conduct an investigation under subsection (1)(a) only if it suspects that the person concerned may have committed an unlawful act.

(3) A suspicion for the purposes of subsection (2) may (but need not) be based on the results of, or a matter arising during the course of, an inquiry under section 16.

(4) Before settling a report of an investigation recording a finding that a person has committed an unlawful act or has failed to comply with a requirement or undertaking the Commission shall—

(a) send a draft of the report to the person,

(b) specify a period of at least 28 days during which he may make written representations about the draft, and

Where the investigation convinces the Commission that the employer has committed an unlawful act, the CEHR may issue an unlawful act notice, which may require the employer to adopt an action plan "for the purpose of avoiding repetition or continuation of the unlawful act." Section 21(4). The employer may appeal the notice to the appropriate court or tribunal.

The CEHR may assist victims who bring suit [Sec. 28(4)]:

In giving assistance under this section the Commission may provide or arrange for the provision of—

(a) legal advice;

(b) legal representation;

(c) facilities for the settlement of a dispute;

(d) any other form of assistance.

Is consolidation of all public enforcement in one body desirable? Is the mix of private and public enforcement effective?

Note: Anti–Discrimination Law and its Enforcement in China

China adopted a Labor Contract law in 1995, which covers collective bargaining, wages and hours, enforcement of contracts, safety and health, non-discrimination, and female/juvenile protective provisions. Although Section 12 provides that "Labourers shall not be discriminated against in employment, regardless of their ethnic community, race, sex, or religious belief," there is no provision for public enforcement of the non-discrimination provisions; Chapter XI does provide for enforcement of other provisions by the labor administrative departments. However, Chapter X, Labor Disputes, seems to provide for mediation and arbitration of discrimination claims. Indeed, a news article reports that a woman who was demoted because she was pregnant won an award of $5,935 from an arbitration panel. "Woman awarded 46,000 yuan for unfair treatment," China Daily, May 8, 2007, p. 6.

After extensive public comment, China in 1997 adopted a law on employment contracts, effective January 1, 2008, designed in part to better protect the interests of workers. Article 3 provides: "The conclusion of employment contracts shall comply with the principles of lawfulness, fairness, equality, free will, negotiated consensus and good faith." It thus includes equality as an element of a more general law. Article 42 places limits on layoffs of disabled and pregnant employees. Article 52 allows collective bargaining agreements to protect "the rights and interests of female employees."

Index

References are to Pages

†